In this book Martin Fid~~~~~~~~~~~~~~~~~~~~
classic murder cases from his late night LBC radio series.
He retells the stories of murders past and present, from
the eighteenth century *cause célèbre* of Mary Blandy to the
1960s atrocity of Michael X. Here are murderers for love
and money, murders within the family and among the
famous, as well as some past mysteries with recent
solutions. Martin Fido garnishes the facts with his
trenchant opinions on the moral aspects, the pathos,
horror or absurdity of the various crimes, to make this
book essential reading for all true crime devotees.

For twenty years Martin Fido taught literature in universities from Oxford to the West Indies. In 1983 he started a new career as a writer and broadcaster, specialising in true crime, and his popular LBC radio programme led to his being described as 'a kind of New Age Edgar Lustgarten'. His book *Murder Guide to London* has provided a basis for a number of tours conducted by City Walks, and he is a leading authority on Jack the Ripper.

*Also by Martin Fido*

The Crimes, Detection and Death of Jack the Ripper
Murder Guide to London

# MURDERS AFTER MIDNIGHT

Martin Fido

ORION

PICTURE ACKNOWLEDGEMENTS

The photographs in this book are reproduced by
permission of the following: The Bethlem
Hospital and The Maundsley Hospital Health
Authority 2; Hulton Deutsch Collection 4, 15;
Mary Evans Picture Library 1, 12, 14; S&G Press
Agency 13; Syndication International 5, 6, 8, 9,
10, 11; and Weidenfeld Archive 3. The
photograph of Friedrich Ritter and Baroness
Wagner-Bosquet (7) comes from *The Galapagos
Affair*, John Treherne (Jonathan Cape, 1983).

An Orion paperback
First published in Great Britain by George Weidenfeld & Nicolson Ltd
in 1990
This paperback edition published in 1993 by Orion Books Ltd,
Orion House, 5 Upper St Martin's Lane, London WC2H 9EA

Second Impression

A CIP catalogue record for this book is available from the
British Library.

ISBN: 1 85797 198 1

Printed and bound in Great Britain by
The Guernsey Press Co. Ltd, Guernsey, Channel Islands.

For Blondie of Tottenham,
Reggie of Brixton,
Sid, the Progressive Skinhead,
the Pimlico Lenin Lads,
and
all the Taxi Drivers

# Contents

# Introduction

In the autumn of 1987, Clive Bull had only recently moved to the weekend Graveyard Shift at LBC Radio: *Through the Night* was just starting to go *Live with Clive*.

There was a good deal of new material on Jack the Ripper emerging at that point, and Clive interviewed me a couple of times to discuss it. After the interviews, we chatted about the difficulties of filling air-time, and the tentative suggestion Gill Pyrah's producer had once put forward for having me discuss murders or crime regularly on her programme, only to have the idea rejected as unfit for family listening. But 1.00 a.m. didn't seem a time when the kiddies were likely to be up having the living daylights scared out of them, and experimentally, three Victorian murders were put down on tape, and 'Murders After Midnight' was born.

When I listened to them broadcast, I was surprised to hear the graceful Tchaikovsky introduction, and learned from Clive that it seemed to him and producer Jonathan Perry that I tended to open with misleadingly sweet and charming descriptions of people and places, and then go on to make listeners sup full of horrors.

I was also surprised to hear myself described as 'Dr' Martin Fido.

Although I taught in universities for twenty years, and have a post-graduate qualification, it is not in fact a doctorate. (The subject, for those listeners who have enquired, was English literature, and my thesis was on Disraeli's novels.) But many people think I am Dr Fido, confusing me, perhaps, with my brother the educational biologist.

It seemed that the conventions of broadcasting forbade me to drop the illicit title. So, enjoying a semi-pseudonym (like Dr Seuss) I felt free to indulge myself in these scripts. From Dr Johnson to

Dr Rowse, it seems to me, doctors have pontificated. I have thoroughly enjoyed garnishing the midnight accounts of horror with the crusted views of opinionated old Dr Fido.

So I was more than a little surprised when a listener coming on one of my crime walks asked whose 'side' I was on: the murderer's or the victim's! I hope the inclusion of such morally indefensible categories as 'Murdered Children' and 'Multiple Murder for Money' will make it clear that I am *always* on the side of the victim. Though the quality of murder differs, and it will usually be found that murders in the former category are distressing, while those in the latter tend to seem comic (because most of us are rather less avaricious than supply-side and competitive economists believe, and find something ludicrous about people who go such a distance in pursuit of profit).

In a period of good true-crime writing, I have included a number of great mysteries and modern solutions. Richard Whittington-Egan, Jonathan Goodman and Bernard Taylor are outstanding professionals in this field. And a splendid new generation is emerging in Kate Clarke, Keith Skinner, Simon Wood and Paul Begg. Nor should one overlook the amateurs who investigate true crime, whether as topographical wanderers like Blondie of Tottenham and her friends, or collectors like Ray Cole and Stewart Evans. Their unpublished opinions may have immense value, and I am delighted to give wider currency to Stewart's reading of the Peasenhall Mystery.

When LBC put out an overnight phone-in on crime early in 1988, I remarked that the moral variations in murder interested me as much as anything. So a section on glamorous celebrities involved in murder looks at the whole business of living in the public eye, and the section on women in love must enforce on us all that romantic love, though delightful and potentially improving, is not in itself morally admirable.

Here then are the prejudiced opinions; the delvings in wickedness; the strange radio-intended punctuation and rhetoric; the edited-out horrors such as what Frederick Baker did to Fanny Adams, in thirty-three of 'Dr' Martin Fido's favourite scripts.

Heamoor/St Katharine's Dock/Gough Square
1987–9

# Part one
# MURDERED PARENTS

# 1

## *Mary Blandy*

Francis Blandy was a lawyer: gentlemanly, thrifty, a little secretive, a bit of a snob. He lived in a comfortable house beside the river at Henley-on-Thames with his wife and grown-up daughter.

Mary Blandy became the toast of the racier set in 1752. Not that the London rakes had met her. But they had all heard of her. That spring, she was one of two women whose names monopolized conversation. She was the more genteel of the two: the more refined and well-educated. Dark-haired and black-eyed (though not unmarked by smallpox) she may even have been the better looking. But she was certainly the older. She was thirty-two when she died. And still unmarried. On the shelf, by Hanoverian standards. And growing a little desperate.

It was not want of looks, manner or graces that kept slender Mary in an unblessed state of spinsterhood. It was her father's peculiar ambition to see her married into a high circle of society that kept driving hopeful young men away. After, moreover, Francis Blandy had deliberately attracted suitors for his daughter with a lure that might even outweigh her personal charms. Unobtrusively, but definitely, Francis let it be known that he was very rich. That he proposed a splendid marriage settlement for his daughter. A dowry of £10,000.

That brought them in while Mary was still young. An apothecary of Henley had always admired her, and hopefully approached Mr Blandy offering his hand. Mr Blandy almost threw the impertinent young pill-dispenser out of his house. The heiress to £10,000 to lock herself forever to a life of High Street medicine peddling! Couldn't Henley's small-town shopkeepers *see* that Mary was worth more than they had to offer?

Nobody else from among the neighbours dared to sue for their townswoman's hand. Mary moved into her middle twenties, still uncourted.

A visit to Bath was Mr Blandy's answer to that. All fashionable England took its recreative vacations there, sampling the waters, and enjoying the flattering and match-making attentions of Beau King, the Master of Ceremonies. And here Mary (or her famous fortune) succeeded in alluring an entirely suitable admirer. A young army officer walked out with her; approached her father; was encouraged; came to a good understanding, and . . . was posted abroad on military duties, passing totally beyond the ken of his sorrowing would-be in-laws at Henley.

A naval gentleman, Captain C—, was the next likely prospect. He strolled beside the river with the yet-relatively-young Mary in a picturesque piece of parkland that was still known as 'Blandy's Walk' 150 years later. Again an agreement was reached, and while Captain C—, too, was ordered out of England on a cruise, there was no doubt that he would be coming back. Alas, when he did, it was tragically clear that he had changed his mind about Mary. Cold courtesy, bare recognition, and no amatory strolls whatsoever comprised his new regimen. Perhaps he had come to doubt the reality of the great Blandy fortune. Perhaps he had noticed a chilling edge of self-interest, calculation and ruthlessness in Miss Blandy's black eye. Either way, he was a wise man, and Francis Blandy showed no inclination to press him to honour his half-spoken commitment.

Mrs Blandy shared her daughter's distress that an ominous thirtieth birthday was approaching, and yet Miss remained obstinately Miss. If Bath had almost succeeded, London might do better. Mother and daughter went for the season to the capital where they plunged into as much of the social whirl as they could afford.

And this time, they really struck lucky. So they thought. Captain the Hon. William Cranstoun was the fifth son of Baron Cranstoun. On his mother's side he was grandson to the Marquess of Lothian, and connected to half the aristocracy of Scotland. His grand-uncle was Lord Mark Kerr, and it was at a reception at his lordship's house that the Oxfordshire heiress met the sprig of Scottish nobility.

They were well-matched. She was past the age of instant attraction. He was dandified, but hardly prepossessing. Short, sallow, decidedly plain, and made worse in his appearance by his extravagant dressiness. But he was an officer and a gentleman. He had served with no particular distinction against Bonny Prince Charlie, and helped 'Butcher' Cumberland crush the Highlands after Culloden. He not merely rubbed shoulders with the nobility, he was one of them. Mrs Blandy's heart was all a-flutter at the thought of a son-in-law who might introduce her to marquesses and marchionesses. Mary, after all her disappointments, would have married a carthorse had one proved eligible and made the offer. Cranstoun might be a frog, but he was a frog with genteel connections. And he was very interested – very interested indeed – in that £10,000.

Mr Blandy was just as pleased as his wife and daughter at first. A genuine pedigreed aristocrat was just what he had hoped for in putting about word of Mary's great expectations. And if Captain Cranstoun tended to borrow money in advance – well! – the dashing eighteenth-century soldier was always a bit of a gambler. You had to pay for style. What would be ne'er-do-well thriftlessness in a small-town tradesman was gentlemanly spirit in a noble half-pay captain. Mr Blandy was so satisfied with the prospect of this traditional union between money and breeding that he pooh-poohed the first warning that all might not be well, though it came from a distinguished, aristocratic and knowledgeable source.

Lord Mark Kerr was distinctly perturbed when he heard that his nephew had gone down to Henley and was staying with the Blandys in the role of prospective son-in-law. The almost-young couple had, after all, met under Lord Mark's roof. He might be held culpable if he failed to warn the lawyer of any impediments to the wedding he planned for his daughter. And Lord Mark knew of a pretty big impediment.

He wrote to Mr Blandy, warning him that Captain Cranstoun was already married.

Here was a blow! Explanations were sought, and from Cranstoun they were quickly forthcoming. His uncle was under an unfortunate misapprehension. True, there was a young woman in Scotland. And she had a baby. Any man of fashion and spirit had that sort of entanglement somewhere in his past, don't y' know? But marriage? Pah! Would a Cranstoun stoop to uniting himself with such a low creature? Certainly not!

He was about to fight the case in the courts to prove that there
was no marriage. Why, he'd even got a letter from the woman
confessing that their liaison never entailed matrimony. What hope
had the silly ambitious thing in going to law in the teeth of such
evidence?

Mr Blandy was convinced. He ignored Lord Mark's warning.
And Lord Mark took umbrage at being slighted by a country
attorney. He ceased to notice the Blandy family.

The case took a long time to wind its way through the Edinburgh
courts. And Cranstoun lost it resoundingly. His undoubted wife
had, indeed, supplied him with a letter averring that they were not
married. He had written her several letters asking for it, and
explaining that as she was a Catholic and her family were
Jacobites, the marriage might hinder his promotion in the army if
it became known. Mrs Cranstoun had kept the letters, and they
convinced the court. Cranstoun was ordered to pay her and her
child alimony. The Scottish legal system evidently thought the
Hon. William was pretty dishonourable: the gallant captain was
pretty much of a jerk.

Still, with impudent volubility, Cranstoun persuaded the
Blandys that this was a mere setback, not an impediment to
marriage. He was going to appeal against the decision, and Mr
Blandy knew, as a lawyer, how often the higher courts overturned
the lower. Of course, since the court had inconveniently declared
that he *was* a married man, the wedding to Mary couldn't take
place until the appeal had been heard and won. But that was a
foregone conclusion. And in the meantime, could he extend his
visit and his enjoyment of the Blandys' hospitality? Oh, and
perhaps another little loan in anticipation of that dowry?

Ultimately it was the sponging and the interest Cranstoun
showed in the dowry that turned Francis Blandy against him. The
proposed bigamy disturbed neither the lawyer, his wife, nor their
daughter. But Cranstoun's insolence and impecuniosity became
tedious. Mr Blandy was quite as unwilling to disgorge the great
inheritance as the captain was to go away and live on his half-pay.
When Mrs Blandy died of a stomach complaint, the lovers lost
their really strong supporter. Francis showed himself more and
more determined that the happy couple should *not* lay hands on the
promised dowry.

The captain's prospects took a turn for the worse when he lost
his appeal. It became necessary for him to go to Scotland and settle

his encumbered affairs. Mary helped him pack, and found some letters proving that, quite apart from the past indiscretion in Edinburgh, there was another woman in London. And he had been keeping her throughout the engagement. Mary was proudly cold. Cranstoun wept and grovelled. She forgave him. And the engagement was still on.

Their love-letters bemoaned the obstacle that Mr Blandy now represented to their nuptial bliss. Mary prudently destroyed most of Cranstoun's, and he never revealed hers. But they certainly discussed the old gentleman, and Cranstoun decided that urgent action was necessary when Mary revealed that he was about to change his will, so that she might never inherit the great fortune.

Cranstoun sent his beloved a present. 'Pebbles from Scotland' – semi-precious cairngorms and topazes that were all the rage in 1751. And he sent her an envelope labelled, 'Powder for cleaning the Scottish pebbles'. But in a letter he told her it was really something else.

It was, he suggested, a love-philtre obtained from an old Highland witch. He had used one himself, some years earlier, when billeted with a gentleman he detested. And, upon his honour, he had felt the greatest kindliness toward his enemy as soon as he had taken the potion. Perhaps, slipped into Mr Blandy's tea, the love-philtre would bring the old gentleman round to looking kindly on his prospective son-in-law.

Mary put some in the tea. The old gentleman was instantly and violently sick. And he declared that the tea had something gritty in it.

Susan Gunnell, the maid, drank a cup of tea Mr Blandy left untouched the following day. She was seriously ill for a week.

Mary changed the vehicle.

Mr Blandy was given nourishing gruel to see him through the illness that had developed from his unpleasant tea. The cook watched Mary prepare it, stir it carefully, and rub her hands over the spoon before stirring it again. She heard Mary call her father a black-hearted old villain, and wish him dead.

Mr Blandy, obligingly, fell increasingly ill. So did old Ann Emmett, the charwoman, when she was allowed to finish up the remains of his meal. The servants and neighbours were suspicious. Mary was making preparations to flee to Scotland when the town clerk visited her and told her she was under arrest on suspicion of trying to poison her father.

Mr Blandy did his best for her. His daughter was 'just a poor love-sick girl,' he said; and he asked, 'What won't a girl do for a man she loves?' But he could not deny that he was being poisoned. And with the local apothecary confirming that his former idol had been putting arsenic in her father's food, the old man died.

Cranstoun fled to the Continent. Mary was tried at Oxford assizes. She admitted that the love-philtre story was a blind devised to protect Cranstoun. Which meant that she had known he was sending something harmful for her father. Which meant that she was guilty of parricide. She was allowed six weeks to set her affairs in order before being hanged outside Oxford Castle.

During this time she corresponded publicly with Elizabeth Jeffries, who was also under sentence of death for parricide. She wrote a pamphlet in defence of her actions, which provoked a pamphlet war, for and against her. Her defenders praised her gifts and graces so highly that she became the toast of London's roués.

Her father's estate proved to be a mere £4,000. This encouraged some sympathy for her, as a poor pawn in his scheme to ally his family with the nobility by trickery.

And finally she went to her death with the words which have made her famous for her unshakeable sense of modesty and decorum under trying circumstances. As she started up the ladder to the scaffold, she realized that the beam fixed between two trees which served Oxford as a gallows was placed very high up. And she became acutely conscious that (like all eighteenth-century ladies) she wore no drawers. And unlike most, she was likely to be left in a state of suspense where lewd youths could stroll underneath her.

'For decency's sake, gentlemen,' she pleaded, 'don't hang me high!'

# 2

# Elizabeth Jeffries
# and John Swan

In the spring of 1752, while the beaux tittered and raised their glasses to Mary Blandy who had poisoned her father for opposing her marriage, another case that had been pending came to trial, and the newspapers throbbed with horror that a second parricide lady should have been exposed. A Bill for the Prevention of the Horrid Crime of Murder was about to go before Parliament. Hanging was laid down for so many trivial crimes, that it seemed necessary to distinguish wilful homicide as rather more heinous than stealing five shillings. And some commentators now seriously suggested that parricides might well be burned to death rather than hanged.

At first sight, the crime of Elizabeth Jeffries did seem peculiarly despicable. The father whose death she plotted was adoptive. Childless Joseph Jeffries and his wife longed for a baby of their own, and in 1732 his brother Thomas, a Shropshire boatbuilder with a large family, consented to make over his little daughter Elizabeth to be brought up by the benevolent couple.

They did their best for her. They tried to educate her in the graces and accomplishments appropriate to the adopted daughter of a prosperous retired butcher in the rural retreat of Walthamstow. But as the years passed, and Elizabeth reached her teens, her bad character came to the fore.

In 1742 she was fifteen, and it became clear that she preferred the card-table to the library. Worse, she was becoming a hardened drinker. Worse still, on a trip to London she met a dashing officer

in a tavern on Tower Hill; ogled him and retired to a private room
in the hope of a lusty debauch, only to be disappointed when the
filthy state of her chemise convinced him that he would not be her
only recent sexual partner, and he refused to run the risk of
contracting a noxious ailment. Good Mrs Jeffries probably never
learned about this escapade, though her 'daughter' must have
been a sad disappointment to her when she died a couple of years
later.

Mr Jeffries now tried to bring Elizabeth to her senses by
lavishing affectionate attention on her and making her his
principal heiress. He made a will leaving her £1,000 clear, his
houses and furniture in Walthamstow and the City, and the
residue of his estate after trifling legacies to other nephews and
nieces had been paid. Elizabeth did not obviously reform.

Nor did she adequately replace her dead foster-mother as a
housekeeper. Around 1748, Mr Jeffries was forced to expand his
household by the acquisition of two servants: a maid called Sarah
Armstrong, and a man called John Swan as general factotum.

Elizabeth lost no time in seducing Swan. By the end of 1750,
their intimate liaison was apparent to Mr Jeffries, who dis-
approved. As the spring of 1751 advanced, he threatened to cut
Elizabeth out of his will if she continued to make an indecent
spectacle of herself. By the early summer, Elizabeth feared that she
would soon make an indisputably pregnant spectacle, and her rich
inheritance seemed to be melting before her eyes.

She was no more willing to renounce Swan than she was to lose
the money. But neither of the lovers was willing to take immediate
personal action to dispose of the old man. Instead, they
approached a poor man called Matthews, who had been employed
by Mr Jeffries for one week to help Swan with the garden. This
tatterdemalion seemed desperate enough to carry out any
nefarious plan for them, and Swan beckoned him into a garden
shed to ask furtively whether he would knock his employer over the
head for him. Elizabeth added her arguments, saying she would
never be happy until 'that old miser her uncle' was dead.
Matthews hesitated, but he was obviously tempted by the promise
of £100, possibly rising to £700 as he still demurred. Neighbours
observed that Elizabeth started urging her foster-father to go out
and drink himself silly at the tavern every night. It seemed just
another mark of her debauched nature.

A decision to change the murder weapon from a cudgel to a pair of pistols took place in May, when Swan went down to London and met Matthews at the Bell Inn in Petticoat Lane. The two were so noisy, and Matthews so ragged, that the landlord searched them, and had them arrested on suspicion of being highwaymen when Swan proved to be carrying heavy horse-pistols. Elizabeth had to leave Walthamstow at 4.00 a.m. and take a carriage in to town to rescue her accomplices from the Bridewell, giving the explanation that the pistols were newly bought, and Swan had been sent to town to have them cleaned.

On 3 July, the plot came to fruition. At 2.00 a.m. several of Mr Jeffries' neighbours heard shots. At 2.45 they were all woken up by Elizabeth hanging out of her bedroom window in her shift, screaming fire and murder. Swan came to the door in his shirt, announcing in some confusion that the house had been robbed, and he feared Mr Jeffries had been murdered. Elizabeth threw herself out of the upstairs window, and scrambled to the ground, twisting her ankle as she did so. Her neighbours (like the gallant captain of Tower Hill) noted with some distaste that her shift was very soiled. She told them that she had seen four men going down stairs, saying that they had done all the harm they could, and now intended to set the house on fire. She feared her father's throat had been cut.

It hadn't. But two shots had been fired into his head, the second from a brittle bullet which had fragmented, making a third deep cut under his ear, which was at first believed to be a knife wound.

Mr Jeffries was not yet dead. But he could not speak or understand questions. A slight pressure of the hand was the most he could manage to show that he knew sympathetic friends were around. And by eight o'clock he passed away.

Elizabeth searched the house and reported that some plate was missing. Swan energetically armed a party with rakes, and they went to drag the pond, where the missing silver was found in a sack. A window beside the back door had been broken, making room for an arm to sneak in and shoot the doorbolt. The whole murderous robbery seemed to explain itself. Those neighbours who remembered the ragged Matthews wondered whether he might have been a party to it: he had been seen around the house that day.

Elizabeth and Swan promptly contradicted each other. One said that Matthews might well know something about the matter, and he had better be looked for. The other said that Matthews was

undoubtedly innocent, and questioning him would only bring
down trouble on the whole household.

Nor was this the only suspicious circumstance. Those neighbours who remembered hearing shots wondered why on earth
Elizabeth had taken three quarters of an hour to raise the alarm.
The murder weapon was obviously one of Mr Jeffries' own pistols,
which were kept hanging in the kitchen as a rule. One was now
missing, but Sarah Armstrong had watched Swan in the kitchen
that very night, shaping lead bullets to fit it, and loading it.
Shavings of lead on the tiled floor confirmed her story.

But it was the broken window that really gave the plot away. It
was one of those picturesque casements, with tiny leaded diamond
panes. The hole had been made with all the care of a fine glazier,
who wanted to ensure that the removal of the panes would not
entail breakage, and all could be made good again with ease. The
leading was carefully rolled back, unbroken. *From the inside!*

A search for Matthews ultimately succeeded, and he confessed
to his part in the plot. On the night of 3 July, Swan and Elizabeth
had handed him a pistol and told him to blow the old man's brains
out. Faced with such stark reality, he refused. They cajoled him
and offered him increasing sums of money; they threatened to kill
him on the spot; finally they told him to go away and never come
back. Only, however, after they made him take a solemn oath
never to reveal a word of their complicity. He took it, but with the
reservation that he could reveal all if his own life was in danger.
Naturally, Matthews became the star prosecution witness.

The trial was delayed long enough for Elizabeth's supposed
pregnancy to prove unreal. She would be hanged for sure,
provided her trial contained no legal error. Few of her contemporaries thought hanging a severe enough penalty for her. And
they continued to believe her a monster of depravity, even though
the court proceedings and the prisoners' confessions after they had
been sentenced to death revealed an extraordinary state of affairs,
casting a quite different light upon the murder. Today we should
have no hesitation in condemning old Mr Jeffries as a villain, and
pitying Elizabeth as his victim!

For the marks of adolescent depravity she evinced were the
direct consequence of his having incestuously corrupted her when
she was only thirteen! When she was fifteen, she found herself
pregnant, and the old man simply hustled her out of the way to
Portsmouth where, by good fortune, she miscarried. A year later

she conceived again. By this time, the deceived Mrs Jeffries was dead, and Joseph refused to deprive himself of his niece's embraces for a gestation period. He procured her an abortifacient, and retained her at home to continue sleeping with him, even as she miscarried. Astonishingly, the moralists of 1752 simply took this distressing incident as evidence that Elizabeth was already the murderess of her foetus, long before she reached adult years.

Once he was widowed, the old lecher made little attempt to conceal his intimacy with his adopted daughter. Her evil reputation in the neighbourhood undoubtedly owed more to the questionable position into which she had been put than to any abnormal appetite for cards and strong waters. The generous legacy was a mere sweetener to keep her docile and stop her from flying back to her innocent parents in Shropshire.

It was Sarah Armstrong, rather than John Swan, who brought a most unhappy situation to a festering head. For the old man took a fancy to her as well. Elizabeth found the two in bed together, and felt hopelessly betrayed. Sarah's wages mysteriously increased. Her clothes became altogether finer and more fashionable than one would expect in an Epping servant. She was evidently becoming Mr Jeffries' first love, and Elizabeth feared that having been ruined morally and emotionally, she might be ruined financially as well if Mr Jeffries altered his will in Sarah's favour, and sent Elizabeth back to Shropshire in unspecified disgrace – confident, like all child-abusers, that his victim's misplaced guilt and shame would conceal his own crime adequately.

In this situation, John Swan seemed like a white knight come to the rescue. Her passion for him was untouched by the stain of incest. Yet still Mr Jeffries insisted that Elizabeth must be his whenever he wanted. It was clear that the occasions when Elizabeth had tried to persuade neighbours to take him out and get him drunk at the tavern were caused by her hope that he might come home too stupefied to ravish her, and not, as had once been believed, to set him up for previous murder attempts. It was even alleged that he had brutally forced her into his bed early on the night when the murder took place.

Swan, of course, did the actual shooting. He confessed to it. But it is a startling consideration that the eighteenth century should have hanged, and strongly wanted to burn alive a woman whom we should almost certainly have given a short or suspended sentence and a course of sympathetic psychotherapy.

# 3

# Sidney Harry Fox

In the previous chapters we looked at women who killed their fathers. Men who kill their mothers are even rarer and, perhaps, nastier. At least Elizabeth Jeffries and Mary Blandy had the excuse of conflicting love affairs. Sidney Fox and Donald Merrett were matricides for no better reason than sheer avarice.

Sidney was a confidence trickster. Not a very successful one. Adolescence as a pretty-boy encouraged him to flutter his eyelids at lonely old ladies, and gentlemen of dubious sexual tastes. Working as a pageboy for an employer who nicknamed him 'Cupid' led him to think that he could get away with various forms of petty theft and deceit, lowering an archly guilty head and batting a long eyelash over his blushing cheek to win forgiveness if he were caught.

This horribly wimpish way of life could not go on for ever. By the time he was thirty-one he had served several gaol sentences. His personal sexual orientation was confirmedly homosexual; but his personality was sufficiently disintegrated that he could also propose dubious matrimony to a woman old enough to be his mother (and, in fact, one of his mother's friends) with the sole intention of defrauding her of her property. His pretty looks had deteriorated to a mop of frizzly hair waving wildly at the edges of an ever-mounting forehead. His wide-set eyes had striven so long to look innocent and ingenuous that they now goggled un-appealingly round, exhibiting a distinct cast.

Sidney's lifestyle was as unlovely as his appearance. He

accompanied his 61-year-old mother from hotel to hotel. They offered false identities; dud cheques; a pathetic lack of luggage and clean clothes. As often as possible they flitted from their hotels leaving unpaid bills. The old lady was as dishonest as her son, but she was to pay dearly for her maternal failings.

In October 1929 the couple wormed their way into the Hotel Metropole, Margate. Sidney had the usual plausible excuses about Passenger Luggage in Advance miscarrying on the railway to explain why he had a single clean shirt by way of possessions, while his mother was somewhat overdressed, with her entire wardrobe on her back. They were admitted, but the manager shrewdly suspected their financial probity, and ordered that their bill should be presented daily. Sidney Fox was at a pretty low ebb.

Unfortunately, he had prospective resources. In April he had taken out a £3,000 insurance policy on the old lady's life. The premium was now falling due, and the shabby fraudster determined to recoup his investment at once.

Twenty minutes before midnight on 23 October the hotel foyer was startled by the spectacle of Sidney racing down the stairs in his shirt sleeves, with no trousers on, shouting that the hotel was on fire. He had a shrewd enough appreciation of the kind of first impression which would distract attention from any appearance of guilt on his part.

Fellow guests and hotel staff hurried upstairs, and saw smoke drifting out from under the closed door of Mrs Fox's room. Sidney appeared too shocked and confused to act helpfully, so another guest struggled in through the smoke, and rescued the partly burned body of the old lady from the chair in which she was sitting. Chair and surrounding carpet had been badly burned, and since his mother had apparently been asphyxiated in the fumes, Sidney was now an orphan and entitled to collect the insurance money. His simulated grief and concern were sufficient to win him a good deal of sympathy from the hotel staff. The suggestion that the old lady had fallen asleep reading in her chair, and dropped her magazine into the gas fire, causing the blaze, seemed probable enough. And the manager's doubts were only reawakened when he heard from other hoteliers in the region that his unfortunate guests sounded very like a pair of swindlers who had been going around leaving a trail of unpaid bills and bad cheques behind them.

Nor was the insurance company especially impressed by an accident claim coming in on a policy that would have expired for want of the second premium due, twenty minutes or so after it occurred. The police looked a little more carefully at the details of this 'accident'.

They were suspicious. Indentations on the bed suggested that the old lady had actually retired before the fire started, and then, somehow, arisen and positioned herself in the burning chair. Might she not have been suffocated first? Sir Bernard Spilsbury, the Home Office pathologist, thought she definitely had. He detected a bruise on her throat, leading him to conclude that someone had killed her as she lay in bed.

The conflagration itself showed no signs of having trailed over to the chair from the gas fire. Instead it was perfectly apparent to trained eyes that it had been deliberately started with petrol-soaked newspapers as tinder. Who could have done this?

Sidney had the motive. And his prompt attempts to collect the insurance showed that he was aware of it. He had the opportunity. He admitted having gone into his mother's room when he smelt smoke, and having panicked when he felt the fumes were overcoming him and he feared that his mother must herself have been overcome.

As he stood trial for his life, he gave one answer that clearly shocked the jury. Why, he was asked, had he closed the door on leaving the room, knowing that his mother was still inside? To stop the fire from spreading into the hotel, he responded. Poor little Cupid! Still thinking that a fetching concern for the public he tried to defraud would win him love and sympathy. But it utterly undercut his alternative pose as the considerate son, concerned first and foremost for his poor mother's well-being.

He didn't waste the world's time by appealing against his conviction. And he was hanged at Maidstone in April 1930.

# 4

# Donald Merrett

What should a concerned and wealthy parent do if a gifted student-age son shows signs of going to the bad? Donald Merrett's mother noted her unstable son's extravagance and passion for female companionship, and decided to keep him under her own observation. She sent him to Edinburgh University so that he could live at home with her, and was gratified to see that he went out regularly to his lectures and classes. Mrs Merrett congratulated herself on having cured her son's tendency to truancy and unreliability.

On 17 March 1926, when Donald was eighteen the two were together at breakfast. Mrs Merrett was going through her mail, and a letter from her bank caused her sharp annoyance. She was rich and methodical, and the suggestion that her account was overdrawn appeared absurd. She went over to her bureau to examine her papers and accounts, preparing to write and ask the bank manager what he thought he was doing.

As she frowned over the discrepancies between the bank's figures and her own, she became aware that Donald was fidgeting behind her. He distracted her from her calculations, and she said smartly, 'Go away, Donald, and don't annoy me.'

What happened next? The twelve good men and true who heard and assessed all the evidence decided that the historical course of events was Not Proven. The certain facts are as follows.

A loud BANG was heard from the breakfast room, followed by Donald's crying out, 'My mother has shot herself!'

Mrs Merrett was found bleeding and unconscious on the floor beside her chair, a bullet wound behind her ear and a pistol by her side.

Donald explained that she had been distressed by her money worries.

Her bank account was, indeed, overdrawn, and the manager's letter was justified.

In hospital when she had recovered consciousness, Mrs Merrett, though not entirely lucid, insisted that she had no money worries, and said that the last thing she remembered was Donald moving restlessly behind her, and then a blinding explosion inside her head.

On 1 April she died. And shortly afterwards, Donald was put on trial for her murder.

As in the case of Sidney Harry Fox, the motive was starkly obvious. Mrs Merrett's bank account was empty because Donald had learned to forge her signature and had cheerfully drawn out all her money to finance his own extravagant dissipation. His reformed life as a student was utterly fraudulent: he had ruthlessly cut lectures and gone to tea-dances and nightclubs where he could meet the young ladies who interested him so much more than academic learning. The bank manager's letter would have brought all those chickens home to roost once his mother had investigated 'her' apparent overspending.

But Donald was saved by forensic science. The prosecution took it for granted that no one would or, indeed, *could* shoot themselves in the back of the head at point-blank range. The unfortunate jury was shown Mrs Merrett's ear on an island of skin, to demonstrate the powder burns that meant the pistol had been held almost touching the head.

But Sir Bernard Spilsbury thought the wound was compatible with suicide, as Donald averred. And, still more strikingly, Robert Churchill, the gunsmith, showed exactly how it could have been done. He held the pistol over his shoulder, pointing directly at his ear. Then, in a quick dramatic movement, he turned his face away from it; and – behold! – the barrel was directed into the back of his head. The jury had the Reasonable Doubt they needed to spare them from hanging a boy for this horrible crime. But rarely can the Not Proven verdict have looked more like its popular translation as 'Go away and don't do it again!'

Donald was, however, jailed for a year for his forgeries. After which he changed his name to Ronald Chesney, and dropped out of sight for twenty years.

He prospered at first, since he came into a large inheritance. He married seventeen-year-old Vera Bonner, spent his way quickly through his money, and deserted her. Until the war, he led the life of a seedy adventurer, barely keeping his head above water by fraud and blackmail.

But wartime suited him splendidly. He joined the Royal Naval Volunteer Reserve, and served without special distinction or disgrace. He came into his own entirely in the post-war occupation of Germany. As one of a ruling military force, entitled to bear arms, and skilled in boat-handling, Ronald Chesney became a leading and successful black marketeer. He adopted a suitably piratical appearance for this, his finest hour. He grew a black beard and sported a gold earring occasionally.

But golden days don't last for ever. The occupation came to an end. Chesney was demobbed. And his criminal talents were not up to maintaining him in the new West German republic. By the end of 1953 he was broke and desperate.

His mind turned to the wife he had abandoned in England. With her mother, the self-styled Lady Menzies, she was running a successful old people's home in Ealing. Chesney had occasionally visited them there, without, of course, ever suggesting that he would return and support Vera. Now it occurred to him that he might enrich himself by Mrs Chesney's death. They had never divorced, so if she died he would inherit her assets. She was known to have alcoholic tendencies, and would undoubtedly be willing to partake of the better part of a bottle of gin, after which her accidental death could easily be staged. Chesney was a man without conscience who had got away with murder once.

He shaved off his beard and donned a pair of spectacles. He took out a passport in a false name, proposing to destroy it the minute he had returned to Germany from his murderous visit to England. He would then be safe, as no evidence would exist that he had ever left Germany.

He travelled to England, and the first part of his plan went entirely as proposed. Vera was drowned in her bath in a haze of gin, and no doubt this would have passed as an accident had matters remained there.

But as he stole out of the house, Chesney encountered Lady Menzies on the stairs. This was unlooked for and disastrous. She recognized him, of course. His false passport and disguise now all went for nothing. Worse, he could now be placed in the house exactly where and when his wife died, and the authorities would be quick to spot that he stood to gain from her death and had made surreptitious entry into the country. Ronald Chesney quickly battered and strangled his mother-in-law to death and headed back to the Continent.

The double murder gave him away at once. Had his plan been less devious, and Vera's body shown signs of foul play, coupled with evidence of a break-in at the house, he might at least have delayed the manhunt. But it was obvious that the intruder who killed Lady Menzies had known his way into and around the building. It became apparent that Vera's accidental death was contrived. It was evident that her husband needed to come forward and declare his innocence and concern. An international police call for Donald Merrett alias Ronald Chesney was put out, as the two murderous identities merged at last under police investigation. And with the law hot on his trail, the rogue put a bullet through his own brain, and ended his inglorious career in a wood near Cologne.

He posthumously supplies the most macabre exhibit in Scotland Yard's Black Museum. For, when the CID asked the West German police for fingerprints from the corpse in the wood, to make sure it really was Merrett, the Germans simply chopped off the arms and despatched them by post. Pickled in a jar, they can be seen to this day.

# 5

# *Richard Dadd*

I learned my cherry-stones from my Victorian grandmother. I didn't learn to say, 'Rich man, Poor man, Beggar-man, Thief.' I learned, 'Tinker, Tailor, Soldier, Sailor, Apothecary, Doctor, Lawyer, Thief.' (Apothecary: the Victorian pharmaceutical chemist.)

Monday, 28 August 1843. Daniel Beauchamp's chaise rolled into the little village of Cobham around six o'clock in the evening. As it approached the Leather Bottle Inn, the elder of his two passengers called to him to stop. The younger disagreed. He wanted the cabman to go further down the high street to The Ship which, he insisted, was the best house in the village.

Beauchamp had been engaged by the two men at Gravesend. The elder was a good-looking man in his fifties, with handsome open features, a rather sharply chiselled nose, and a bald crown surrounded by well-kempt grey hair which only added distinction to his appearance. He was neatly dressed in a black coat and dark trousers, a green plaid waistcoat and trim black shoes.

The younger had a less benign expression. His rather flat, broad face was clean shaven; his very pale blue eyes a little unfriendly. His brown Taglioni overcoat, dark-blue frock coat and light-blue trousers lacked the spruce nattiness characterizing his companion. His insistence prevailed, and Beauchamp took his fares to The Ship, where the elder paid, and both went into the inn.

John Adams, the waiter in the parlour, recognized the elderly gentleman as Mr Robert Dadd, a former apothecary of Chatham who had made a name for himself locally eleven years earlier by his active support for the Reform Bill, and then left the county for London.

Mr Dadd immediately asked the waiter whether they could have beds for the night. Adams told him that The Ship did not offer accommodation, but he could get him put up in some nearby cottages. Did the gentlemen want one bed or two?

'This is my son,' replied Mr Dadd, 'and one bed will be enough.'

But as Adams reached the door, the son growled sharply. 'Get two beds.'

Adams quickly made arrangements with some Cobham cottagers, and came back to tell the Dadds that they could have separate beds if they didn't mind sleeping in separate houses. That, it seemed, would do very well, and Mr Dadd ordered tea for them both.

After serving them, Adams went back to the cottages to confirm that the beds were taken. On his return, father and son had gone out for a walk, from which they did not return for about an hour. When they came in, Robert Dadd ordered broiled ham for himself, and biscuits and cheese with a pint of porter for his son. At half-past eight, Adams came in to see if they wanted anything else. He heard young Dadd say to his father, 'Will you go for a walk?' to which the older man replied that he was tired and had walked enough. The young man then went quickly out of the parlour and into the bar where Mrs Emma Matthews, the publican's wife, was serving. He abruptly asked for a glass of water, and drank two in quick succession. She noticed that his gaze wandered as his head swayed from side to side, and his manners were not quite what she would expect of a gentleman. But she thought little of it.

Back in the parlour, Adams found the glass of porter was untouched.

'Doesn't your son like porter,' he asked.

'I don't know, I'm sure,' was the reply, in a very melancholy voice, after which Dadd chatted generally to the waiter as an old acquaintance, without any further reference to his son.

His melancholy and his silence were easily explicable. The Dadds were a close and loving family, and young Richard's recent return from the Mediterranean had proved no cause for rejoicing. Perhaps the sun, perhaps the strange experience of foreign crowds, and almost certainly some hereditary predisposition, had affected his mind. His travelling companion felt unsafe with him by the time they returned to France. English doctors confirmed that he was unstable and dangerous. Now his affectionate father was keeping him company at all times, and had brought him on the short outing to Cobham to give the young man a break from work in London, and to talk sympathetically about his future. But not even Robert Dadd suspected that in his son's disordered mind he was coming to figure as, 'The man who calls himself my father'. No one suspected that Richard Dadd believed himself under the personal direction of the ancient Egyptian god Osiris, charged with a vital mission.

At the end of the conversation Robert Dadd ordered a whisky and water for himself. Adams left him with it as the young man came back into the room at a quarter to nine. He evidently renewed his invitation for a walk in the last fading daylight, for Mrs Gardner saw the pair leave the house before half-past nine.

They walked out of the village to Cobham Park, seat of the Earl of Darnley. They took a circuitous route around the Hall which brought them to a gravel pit about thirty yards inside the park off Halfpence Lane. There were trees overhanging the pit, and the spot was clearly in view from both the Hall and the road by day. But in the dusk of that August evening, they were effectively quite alone and invisible.

Mr Robert Dadd turned quietly toward a tree and started unbuttoning his trousers to relieve himself. As he did so, quite unexpectedly, his son attacked him with frenzied ferocity. The older man threw up his hands to defend himself, but a heavy blow to the right side of his head knocked his hat off and momentarily stunned him. More blows rained on his chest, and his hat was trampled in the scuffle. As he fell to the earth, his son seized his coat collar and dragged him under the low branches of the trees which nearly swept the ground beside the gravel pit. There the young man took a brand new and unusually large razor from his pocket and attempted to cut his father's throat. The coat, dragged up over the old man's ears, obstructed him, and he only succeeded in slashing the lapel and lightly cutting the left side of his neck.

Quickly throwing down the razor he took another weapon from his pocket: a large new seaman's spring-bladed knife. With this he stabbed at his father's heart, missing it, but piercing the skin high on the chest near the shoulder. A second thrust passed between the ribs and into the lung. The mortal blow penetrated the lung to a depth of four inches, and the knife was turned and thrust in again

before it was removed. Mr Dadd's coat had been pulled so high
over his head as he was dragged to his resting place that all the
stab-wounds passed entirely below it, tearing only his waistcoat
and shirt.

Richard had carried out the command of Osiris. He had killed
Satan after the fiend had assumed the guise of 'the man who calls
himself my father'.

Leaving his father lying on his face, gasping and bleeding to
death, Richard Dadd hurried to the stile leading into Hall Road.
He dropped his bloody knife ten yards from the body, and swung
himself over the stile, leaving crimson handprints on its top rung.
And away into the dusk he raced.

With him into darkness passed his prospects as one of the most
successful young painters of his generation. He was a fellow-
student of Augustus Egg and William Frith, and the first of the
three to achieve commercial success. Dadd's charming and
decorously sexy Victorian fairy paintings often took subjects from
Shakespeare: 'Puck', 'Titania Sleeping', 'Come Unto These
Yellow Sands'. Before taking his fateful outing to Cobham, he had
shut himself up in his studio in London, surrounded with hundreds
of hard-boiled eggs and bottles of beer, so that cooking and eating
need not distract him from the easel. But in the studio were
portraits of all his friends, with sinister red lines drawn across their
throats.

Thirty yards from Halfpence Lane the body lay still, covering
the razor. Robert Dadd's bruised and bloodstained face, bruised
wrists, slashed thumb and mangled chest were concealed. To all
appearances, a gentleman had decided to take a nap *al fresco*,
snuggled under his coat collars. So thought a passing butcher who
noticed it in the morning. And was deeply shocked to find a dead
man covered with blood.

Richard had fled to Dover, where he hired a small boat to take
him to France. He took a coach from Calais to Paris, and cast
unfriendly eyes on the English working man who travelled with
him. He spent a day in Paris buying new travelling things, before
taking the *diligence* to Valence. Once there, he booked a seat for the
long stage-coach journey to Vienna.

Between Montereau and Langres, Osiris spoke to him again.
Richard made two light passes with his razor over the throat of the
harmless Frenchman travelling with him, and finally started
trying to kill him in earnest. This was no lonely gravel pit. The man

cried out and the coachman pulled Dadd off him. He was sent to the asylum at Melun, and thence to Clermont-Ferrand, where he spent ten months. The French were unwilling to permit the extradition of a lunatic, but finally accepted that the English did not intend to hang Dadd, but only to prove his insanity before the courts, and then place him in an asylum where his family might more easily have access to him. Dadd went straight from the magistrates' court to Bedlam, and was lost to the sight of his contemporaries.

But when the new asylum for criminal lunatics was opened at Broadmoor, Dadd was moved to its more comfortable surroundings. There his art blossomed again, and he painted his most remarkable works. He died peacefully in 1886 at the age of sixty-eight, almost forgotten by the artistic world.

In the 1960s, Patricia Allderidge, the archivist of the Tavistock Clinic which inherited the old Bethlehem Hospital files, discovered this remarkable ex-inmate. She brought serious scholarly attention to his work and organized a great exhibition of his fairy paintings, fantastic landscapes, haunting portraits and puzzle pictures.

Today the Tate Gallery houses Richard Dadd's chef d'oeuvre: 'The Fairy Feller's Master-Stroke'. It was painted in the years of his madness with an obsessive precision and detail. A crowd of elves and goblins watch, as a fairy wood-cutter swings his felling-axe to split a hazel-nut. At the top of the picture, a row of gnome-like creatures represent their nursery-rhyme occupations . . . Tinker, Tailor, Soldier, Sailor, Apothecary . . . .

Yes, apothecary. And there, hard at work among his flasks and bottles is the elfish likeness of Robert Dadd, tragic victim of a tragic son.

# 6

## Lizzie Borden

Fall River, Massachussetts, the New England town on the border with Rhode Island, has inspired several books, a ballet, and a couple of masterly essays from the doyen of American true-crime, Edmund Pearson. And it gave us the famous rhyme that everyone knows. . . .

> Lizzie Borden took an axe
> And gave her mother forty whacks.
> And when she saw what she had done,
> She gave her father forty-one.

Andrew Borden was a successful, dour parsimonious business-man in the late nineteenth-century New England mode. He had interests in many ventures in Fall River, and in the world of trade and commerce his name was good. He was enterprising: what the Thatcher government used to call a self-starter, or 'one of us'.

At home he was a ghastly example of what middle age does to the successful philistine materialist. He lived with his second wife and two grown-up daughters by his first marriage. The women of the family went to church, of course. But religion was not really important in their lives. The arts had no place whatsoever. The one interest turning the wheels of the household was making, hoarding and cautiously spending money. (Or, as they would have said, in traditional Protestant ethical terms, working hard and prospering.)

It was a joyless prosperity. They lived in an ugly two-storey wooden frame house filled with ugly horsehair stuffed furniture. They kept one Irish maid. They positively reeked of the inability to have any *fun*, and of a humourless incomprehension of those who did.

It's a wonder they ever said grace, for the food served up in the Borden household was such a thrifty compilation of warmed-over and reshaped leftovers of leftovers that it had usually been so frequently blessed it might as well have left for heaven then and there.

The first week of August 1892, was the joint of mutton week. It arrived first as a hot joint. It reappeared as cold cuts, as mutton soup, and hashed in patties – oh, the mutton on its own might well have caused a murder!

Miss Lizzie's older sister was away visiting friends, and missed the excitement of 4 August. To compensate, John Vinnicum Morse, the girls' uncle was visiting. Bridget the Irish maid was feeling sick, as well she might, with the increasingly elderly mutton undergoing its endless resurrections. Mrs Borden set her to clean the windows on the outside of the house. Bridget spent the morning labouring round the great wooden-frame box with bucket and washcloth.

Mrs Abbie Borden was a stout household drudge who had been pretty undisguisedly married by the widowed Andrew as a needful piece of furniture to look after his daughters and his home comforts. She had equally undisguisedly married him for the security and income he represented. You can no more imagine *love* or *romance* between those two than you could between any two members of a pre-Gorbachev Supreme Soviet.

Mrs Borden's domestic tasks took her upstairs that morning, in the front part of the house where she and Mr Borden slept opposite the guest bedroom, quite apart from Miss Lizzie's room at the back of the house. Miss Lizzie had never hidden her dislike of her stepmother; her feeling that her own daughterly financial inheritance was threatened by this interloper. Miss Lizzie lived her life as much to herself as the house permitted.

Uncle John Vinnicum Morse had gone into town to visit friends – he seems to have been a little more sociable and human than his Borden relatives. Bridget washed windows. Miss Lizzie sat in her room at the back of the house doing . . . whatever Miss Lizzie was doing.

Around midday Mr Borden came home. He had visited his various enterprises, and grimly made sure that the wheels of commerce were revolving in his favour. Miss Lizzie came downstairs, and her father asked where his wife was. Miss Lizzie said she had gone out to visit a sick neighbour. Miss Lizzie didn't recall who or where.

Andrew made little response, though he probably felt his womenfolk should be available to serve *him*, not gadding about serving God or humanity. He took off his coat and put his feet up on the uncomfortable sofa in the dining-room to enjoy forty winks before lunch. Bridget had finished the windows and gone to her room to lie down. Miss Lizzie was . . . wherever Miss Lizzie was.

About twenty minutes later she called out to Bridget for help. Someone had come in and killed Mr Borden. There he lay on the sofa, dreadfully battered by an axe. Bridget had heard nothing. Miss Lizzie had heard nothing. But the door in from the garden had been ajar with only the insect screen door across. Evidently some strange enemy had intruded.

Neighbours came in answer to the cries for help, and found Bridget panicky; Miss Lizzie undetermined about what to do, yet curiously self-possessed. Nobody expected paroxysms of grief from a Borden.

Some neighbours set off to look for Mrs Abbie Borden on her charitable errand – Miss Lizzie didn't know exactly where. Others sent for the police. Two courageous souls went up the front stairs. (Miss Lizzie's courage failed her at that point, and she would not accompany them.) As their heads ascended above the landing floor level, they could glance through the open door of the guest bedroom. There they saw poor stout Mrs Abbie Borden lying battered on the floor between the bed and the wall. The famous rhyme is wrong about one thing. Mrs Borden was struck more often and with greater savagery than her husband.

Now here was a mystery. Who on earth could have done it?

Uncle John Vinnicum Morse arrived home and proved himself a true member of a thoroughly respectable New England family. He paid no attention to the knot of bystanders outside the house, but went quietly into the garden on his own, picked a windfall pear, and ate it.

Suspicion fell on him for this strangely uncurious behaviour. Uncle John had witnesses to prove exactly where he had been all morning, and it was never in or near the house. Suspicion had to go away again.

After a few days it settled on Miss Lizzie. She had been in or around the house all morning, and gave inadequate and self-contradictory explanations of what she had been doing. She had suddenly changed from the blue dress she had been wearing when Andrew came home for lunch, into a brown dress. And a few days later she had been seen burning a blue dress in the basement boiler. Wasn't this getting rid of bloodstained garments?

In that basement the police found a hatchet which could have been the murder weapon. Something like a bloodstain remained on the blade, but it had been recently scrubbed clean with ashes. Nobody admitted to carrying out this scouring.

After a lot of hesitation, Miss Lizzie was finally charged with murdering her father and stepmother. She told an improbable story which should have hanged her on the spot. She said that while the assailant crept into the house, she had been up in the loft over the Bordens' barn in the garden, selecting pieces of iron to make sinkers for fishing at the church picnic next weekend.

Cor! That was an obvious whopper! No one had ever heard of either of the Borden girls fishing, let alone on church picnics! Nobody since Lizzie Borden has weighted their lines with lumps of iron rather than split lead shot. And anyway, there was no iron whatsoever in the loft. Instead, as an immediate police search of the premises had established, there was an unbroken carpet of dust that must have lain building up over months, untrodden by anyone.

But that immediate police search helped Miss Lizzie in the matter of the blue dress. They had examined all the clothes and cupboards in the house, including Miss Lizzie's, and failed to detect a trace of bloodstained clothing. (It took Victoria Lincoln, the first woman writing on the case, to point out that she would always know how to conceal a dress from prying masculine eyes simply by putting it on a hanger inside another one.)

Most of all, Lizzie was helped by her trial lawyer. Ex-Governor Robinson was a highly respected Massachussetts politician. With controlled New England courtesy, he simply treated it as impossible that a lady could have done such a thing. 'Look at her, gentlemen!' he implored the jury.

They did. They considered the town's reputation. They found her not guilty.

But the townsfolk knew Lizzie had quarrelled with her family over her stepmother's inheriting property from Andrew Borden's hoard. They knew she had tried to buy prussic acid earlier that month. They were sure that she was actually guilty. They kept it discreetly in the Fall River family, however, simply forbidding their children to speak to Miss Lizzie for the remainder of her life on the genteelly understated ground that, 'She was rather unkind to her parents, dear!'

# Part Two
# MURDERED CHILDREN

# 1

## Esther Hibner

Women servants who kill their employers after quarrels are not uncommon: Mrs Merrifield, Kate Webster and Marguerite Diblanc all come to mind. Even Lizzie Borden, the American *nonpareille*, almost had her infamy stolen from her by a researcher who claimed that Bridget, the family maid had actually taken the axe that gave the Borden parents their forty whacks. In real life, as opposed to detective fiction, 'The maid did it!' is more likely than 'It was the butler!'

But the converse can also happen. Women are more likely than men to become outraged with their servants and punish them to death. In eighteenth-century Mayfair, Sarah Metyard and her daughter became so exasperated with their maid, Ann Naylor, that they tied her up in a standing position and let her die of exhaustion and starvation. Across the town, in a court off Fleet Street, Elizabeth Brownrigg flogged and starved Mary Clifford to death. These cases are always distressing: always instances of reasonably prosperous well-nourished women with family backing bullyragging, humiliating, under-feeding and finally destroying the pathetic waifs and orphans who supplied cheap domestic labour before the merciful invention of the vacuum cleaner.

The most distressing of all is the case of Esther Hibner.

She was a business woman – far from an unknown status until mid-Victorian sentimentality suggested that women could aim at nothing better than being plushy, cuddly, chocolate-boxy, churchy mothers of families, and that the sacred calling of motherhood left no space for any other central activity. Esther's business was tambour-frame embroidery work: elegant patterns of flowers, and curlicues and geometrical figures for antimacassars and napkins; personal initials and crests and mottoes for the fine linen of the gentry. Beautiful hand-wrought ornamentation of the pre-industrial age: the sort of craftsmanship we look at in museums and old churches, and wish we could find being made today. We forget how it was made.

This kind of work barely supported a single person at subsistence level. Esther had a daughter, Esther junior. And neither had any intention of wearing their fingers to stumps with the embroidery needle in return for mouldy crusts. They employed a forewoman, Ann Robinson, and, in the absence of any machinery, set up a sweat shop.

The ratepayers of 1828 had no wish to support the old, the unemployed, the indigent or the orphaned if the free market and the private sector could be made to do it for them. It seemed an excellent principle that people should be offered work, rather than charity or a dole. The parish officers were sent out to find employers for the orphans in their care. We all remember Mr Bumble the Beadle dragging Oliver Twist out for sale to a brutal sweep, and finally to the uncongenial undertaker, Mr Sowerberry.

Esther Hibner went down in the records as a parish benefactor. She could employ no less than six poor orphan girls, finding them food and clothing and shelter. None of them was older than eleven. The cost of their maintenance was taken off the ratepayers' expenses. They were freed from the great grim workhouse, and released into Esther's private house in Camden Town. They were bound apprentice to her: articled to work for seven years while they learned their trade.

And work the little girls did. The notorious dark satanic mills of the north country were sluggardly by comparison. At 3.30 a.m. the working day began. At 11.00 p.m. it ceased. Four hours of refreshing sleep, and the next day's labour started. This gruelling routine was essential if the little girls' efforts were to support themselves, the two Hibners, and their immediate taskmistress, Ann Robinson.

We may question how well the little girls actually slept, whatever their exhaustion. Their bed was the stone floor of Esther's unheated cellar. Their bedding was one single blanket between them. Not surprisingly, they tended to nod off during the

daytime. Their employers had an answer for this problem. Ann
Robinson kept a set of canes, and at hourly intervals the children
were flogged into wakefulness and set back to stitching the elegant
adornments of the gentry.

Growing girls needed proper nourishment for such an arduous
training in the difficult life that lay ahead of them. Esther's
provision was regular and prudent but hardly adequate. She
bought half a pint of milk a day. At 6.00 a.m. she and her daughter
and Miss Robinson took what they wanted of it in their tea. What
was left was then distributed between the six little apprentices.
They were each given a slice of dry bread at the same time. This
was their breakfast.

The remainder of their diet was potatoes. Esther bought 9 lbs a
week and shared among them. Each child, thus, received less than
a quarter of a pound a day. Every other Sunday was their red-letter
day, when they also received a single thin slice of meat.

This utterly evil regimen would probably have killed all of them
before many years were out. But Frances Colpitts, smallest and
weakest of the girls, was quite unable to maintain the high
standard of workmanship demanded in the sweatshop. To punish
her, one day, young Esther picked her up by the heels, and held
her, head downward in a bucket of water. When she pulled her out,
gasping and choking, Ann Robinson screamed, 'Damn her! Dip
her again and finish her!'

It would have taken little to do so. The cold, malnutrition and
misery worked quickly on the child's constitution, and abscesses
formed on her lungs. As it became harder for her to breathe, even
the Hibners realized that she was actually ill and not merely
malingering. So they were embarrassed when Frances's grandmother turned up at the door saying she wanted to visit the little
girl. The Hibners explained that the child had been naughty, and
they were not allowing her any visitors for the time being. This was
not a normal condition of apprenticeship, and the old lady
indignantly reported her rebuff to the parish authorities.

And now that despised parochial official, the beadle, came into
action in a properly protective role. He called on the Hibners and
insisted on seeing the children he had placed in their care. He was
appalled. They were ragged, frozen and starving. All were covered
with lice. Frances was seriously ill and receiving no treatment. The
good Bumble immediately rushed them back to the workhouse,
where the notorious diets were generous and nutritious by

comparison with the rations they had received from private sector
benevolence. Little Frances was put straight to bed, to receive
sympathetic care and attention from paupers and officials, united
in horror at her condition.

Alas, it was too late. She died within a few days in the infirmary.

Her wicked employers went on trial for her murder in February
1829. There was no doubt the jury would have liked to hang all
three of them, but the judge had to tell them, regretfully, that the
circumstances made this impossible as the law then stood. Only
the immediate cause of the child's death was actual murder. If they
felt that this immediate cause was the dipping in cold water, then
Esther Hibner senior could not be hanged, for she had played no
part in it. If the death resulted from malnutrition, exhaustion and
cold, then Esther alone was responsible as the owner and
paymistress of the business.

Regretfully the jury decided that the supreme penalty must be
awarded to the author of the system, and Esther went unlamented
to the gallows. Her daughter and Ann Robinson were sent back to
prison while the law hunted for other charges to bring against
them. Personally, I hope they were transported at the very least.

# 2

## Frederick Baker

Sweet Fanny Adams. You probably think of it as a euphemism, deriving from Sweet F.A., nothing, worthless. The initials of sweet f . . . all. They tell me on LBC Radio that someone will complain if I fill in the word beginning with 'f'. All right. But I say, 'F . . . all' quite happily in private life, and think it far less offensive than the term Sweet Fanny Adams, which actually preceded it.

She was seven and a half years old. Had long fair hair and blue eyes. A pretty little child. Sweet indeed.

On a hot Saturday in August 1867, her father, a bricklayer, was playing cricket as became a good Hampshire man. Her mother was working in the kitchen, and told Fanny to take her little sister Lizzie and go play in the meadow near the River Wey, beside the town of Alton where they lived. Fanny and Lizzie met Minnie Warner, another little girl of Fanny's age, and the three romped happily in the long grass near a part of the field they called the hollow. They made a fetching picture, and it caught the eye of a young man who was taking time off his work to stroll through the fields himself. A very respectable-looking young man. The image of a decent Victorian, uncomfortably attired despite the hot weather. He had a neat black coat, a light waistcoat and light trousers. His tall black hat came steadily over the meadow toward the children.

He didn't offer them sweets. He offered ha'pennies. A ha'penny each for Fanny and Lizzie if they would run down into the hollow for him. The girls happily agreed. Another ha'penny if they would come into another part of the field where he would pick berries for them. Again they were happy to do so.

Now would Fanny come on her own into the nearby hop plantation with him? This time the girls were less certain. The young man solved the problem easily. Giving Minnie and Lizzie another ha'penny apiece, he told them to run along home while he picked up Fanny playfully and carried her into the hops.

Lizzie and Minnie tripped away to Alton chattering about their adventure. When she arrived home Lizzie brightly told her mother about the nice man who had given the girls coppers. Mrs Adams was naturally perturbed. Apart from the whole principle of taking presents from strangers, a nasty old man had recently been lurking around the district trying to persuade children to let him take indecent liberties with them in return for pennies. Mrs Adams took a neighbour for moral support and went to look for Fanny and the strange man.

When he came out of the meadow to the road they accosted him angrily. He was polite and reassuring. He had given the children coppers in fun, and left them to make their own way to the gate. He willingly told them who he was and where they might find him. He was Frederick Baker and he worked for a firm of solicitors in town. They would find him there any time they wanted. He was just on his way back to work now.

The women were reassured. He looked respectable and spoke politely. He wasn't the old man other children had reported. And a molester would hardly give them directions to find his employers. They let him pass, and Frederick Baker went on his way to have some beer for tea before returning to the office. There a fellow-clerk named Biddle chaffed him on the length of time he had been out having his tea.

And still Fanny was not to be seen. A thorough-going search could not be instituted until Mr Adams arrived home from cricket. At seven o'clock it started.

At the entrance to the hop plantation they found the first intimation of tragedy. A good deal of blood.

Just inside the plantation lay Fanny's little blue cotton dress, torn and bloodstained. But it took some searching before they found the first real horror. Fanny's head was stuck on a hop-pole, the eyes gouged out and one ear torn off. A little way away lay the upper half of her torso, with the heart scooped out. A big stone, with some of Fanny's long blonde hair bloodily stuck to it was evidently a weapon with which the assault had started. Further miserable hunting uncovered an arm. And, as darkness fell, her heart, discarded some way away from the head and thorax.

Next day Fanny's other arm was discovered, the ha'penny still clutched in her tiny hand. In a field of clover, one of her feet had been dropped. It seemed that other parts must have been thrown in the river, which ultimately yielded her eyes, but not the abdomen which might have confirmed the obvious suspicion that the poor child had been raped as well as dismembered.

Mr Adams and his friends wanted to lynch Frederick Baker, and who shall blame them? But the authorities arrested him, put him securely in Winchester Gaol, and brought him to trial.

The evidence lay heavily against him. He had commented to his fellow-clerks that it would go hard with him if the missing girl should prove to have been murdered. Then he claimed that he was drunk when he said it, and had been drunk when he spoke to the women outside the meadow. It was observed that his boots and trouser bottoms were soaking wet as though he had washed them thoroughly. He agreed that this was true, but remarked that he often walked through dew in long grass and had to wash them. An odd observation, given that his long walk had been taken in the middle of a sweltering afternoon.

But more sinister than his trousers were his cuffs and wristbands. They were bloodstained. Not only could Baker give no explanation for this, but he remarked himself that he didn't see any scratches on his hands or arms. A modern criminologist might take this as an over-sophisticated attempt to prove that he had not received any defensive injuries from a rape victim. But it is quite clear that Baker was simply joining his questioners in expressing surprise that the blood did not seem to be his own.

There were two knives in his possession, and one of them had bloodstains on it. The knives were rather small – too small, Baker argued – for dismembering a little girl. But poor Fanny had been very small, too.

The most damning evidence of all was a diary hidden away among the papers on his desk. It bore the chilling entry, 'Saturday August 24th. Killed a young girl. It was fine and hot.'

The bulk of the townsfolk wanted to tear Baker limb from limb, even as he had torn Fanny. But Biddle and his fellow-clerks were honestly willing to give him as much credit as truth permitted. While their evidence showed that he had been out of the office an

unconscionably long time that afternoon, and seemed to be
announcing his innocence of any murder even before it was known
that one had been committed, they also felt that he had not had the
opportunity to make the diary entry and hide it in their presence,
and so testified before the magistrates.

Logically this would mean that the police had forged the entry in
order to ensure a conviction – an utterly unlikely hypothesis, given
that any Hampshire jury was going to convict Baker out of hand,
with a rider that he should be drawn and quartered if the judge
would permit. In any case, Baker admitted, first that it seemed to
be in his handwriting, and later that he had in fact written it.
Though according to him all it meant was, 'A young girl was killed.
The day was fine and hot.'

His friends told the court of his depression and fits of strange
conduct ever since a young woman had broken off her engagement
to him. They described nosebleeds and fainting fits that had
impeded his work. And there was evidence that some streak of
hereditary madness ran in his family. But this could not save him
under the old Macnaughton Rules defining exculpatory madness.
These insisted that only a mental illness which prevented the
criminal from knowing that what he was doing was wrong could be
accepted for an insanity plea. In Macnaughton's own case, for
example, the poor man had been making an amazing nuisance of
himself to the Edinburgh authorities for years, complaining that
alternatively the Jesuits, the Catholics or the Tories were plotting
to kill him. He even fled to France to escape the blood-plot, but
found that the other side of the Channel, too, was populated by his
mysterious murderous enemies. So that when he shot Sir Robert
Peel's secretary it was part of a longstanding illness, and in his own
mind he was acting in self-defence. When his judges heard that the
prosecution were bringing no rebutting evidence against the clear
testimony to Macnaughton's delusions, they stopped the trial and
had Macnaughton sent straight to an asylum. Similarly, Richard
Dadd showed no remorse after killing his father; did not deny his
crime; and clearly intended to go on attacking incarnations of the
evil one under the delusion that this was his divinely inspired
mission unless he were prevented.

But Baker obviously knew that what had been done to Fanny
Adams was wrong. His public appearances were the signal for
vehement and understandable execrations, and these clearly
frightened and distressed him. He did not glory in his notoriety.

Rather, he obstinately and hopelessly denied his involvement.
Baker was convicted and hanged, though obviously, loathsome as
his crime was, we should be bound to call him a madman today.

And how did this really tragic story become the basis of a half-
obscene jocularity for nothing or something worthless? The black
humour originated in the navy when tinned rations were introduced. The apparent uncertainty as to what this anonymous and
unpalatable food might be cut from led some wag to suggest that
the meat was Sweet Fanny Adams. Later this shortened to sweet
F.A. And then it was observed that the poor child's initials might
equally stand for f . . . all. Well, the latter is an expression I will use
quite cheerfully. But you won't catch me calling something
worthless 'Sweet Fanny Adams'. That's really obscene. Don't you
agree?

# 3

## Jeannie Donald

Murder is rare: child murder, thank heaven, is extremely rare. When it occurs, the natural suspicion is that the murderer was a man and the motive was sexual. Yet women do sometimes kill children. The motives are rarely clear, but frequently seem related to a wearing life-style in crowded tenements or high density public housing. From time to time, it seems, a woman may kill a neighbour's child in a fit of vexation. One such, who also made her crime look like a man's sexual assault, was Jeannie Donald.

She was thirty-eight in 1934, when she lived in a two-room flat on the ground floor of a tenement in Urquhart Road, Aberdeen. She was married with a nine-year-old daughter; her husband Alexander worked in a hairdressing salon.

The family did not mix much with neighbours in the tenement, and Mrs Donald was in some way disliked and teased by eight-year-old Helen Priestly who lived in the flat above. Helen used to ring the Donalds' doorbell cheekily as she skipped out of the building. When Mrs Donald gave herself a rather unsuccessful home perm, leaving her hair frizzy instead of wavy, little Helen jeered, 'Coconut!' at her. From such childish provocation in cramped quarters, tragedy may spring.

On 20 April, Helen came home from school in the dinner hour as usual. After lunch she was sent out to buy a loaf from the baker's. She bought it; took a receipt; was seen making her way home with it at 1.45; and was never seen alive again.

By two o'clock when afternoon school started, Mrs Priestly was worried that her daughter had not returned with the loaf. By 3.00 she knew that she had not been seen at school all afternoon, and the police started a search. At 6.00 p.m. they got their first clue. A nine-year-old boy told them that he had seen Helen being taken on a tram by a man in a dark overcoat. A district-wide search followed. Helen was described on the wireless and in messages flashed across cinema screens. But by midnight there was still no further clue.

At half-past four in the morning Mr Alexander Porter who lived opposite the Priestlys got up. Downstairs in the hallway he saw a sack in a dark corner. A child's legs were sticking out from it. Helen had been found.

But the finding was mysterious. The sack had definitely not been there at midnight when a final search of the staircases, hallways, lavatories and other public areas of the tenement house had been made. If a man in an overcoat had abducted the child on a tram, why on earth had he brought her back in the small hours to dump her body outside her own home? Why had nobody seen a man with a sack out on the streets anywhere that night?

On the other hand, the body showed clear signs of having been assaulted by a man. Helen's school beret and knickers were missing, though her other clothes remained on her. And rough injuries in and around her genitals showed that she had been raped. The cause of death was strangulation *after* the sexual assault. The search for the man in the overcoat was redoubled.

The question whether or not he owned a car became important. He had, apparently, taken Helen a tram-ride's distance from home in the first instance. Yet in the hours between midnight and 4.30 a.m., when he returned the body, there had been heavy rain, and the sack and the body were both dry. Under renewed questioning, the boy who had seen Helen abducted burst into tears and admitted he had made the whole story up.

Now the focus of the enquiry came firmly back to the tenement building in Urquhart Road. It seemed probable that the dry body and the dry sack had never left the building. All the occupants gave the police details of their movements after the school dinner hour on 20 April. Alexander Donald said he had been at work. Jeannie said she had gone shopping, and returned home soon after 2.00 p.m. to spend the afternoon ironing her daughter's dance frocks ready for a rehearsal at dancing school that evening.

A search of the flats in the building threw immediate suspicion

on the Donalds. There were nine sacks in their room. Five of them
had holes in one corner, exactly like the sack in which Helen's body
had been found. Three of them had black rings made by saucepan
bottoms which had been stood on them. Again, there was just such
a ring on the sack which had held Helen.

The forensic scientific laboratory examined the dust and fluff in
the bottom of the sack. It contained over two hundred different
fibres, including wool, silk, cotton, cat and rabbit hairs, and some
human hair. The composition exactly matched a sample of
household dust taken from the Donalds' floor. The human hair
had been badly permed, and matched a sample of Jeannie
Donald's hair. A few cinders in the sack and some cinder grit
between Helen's teeth proved to have been washed. Mrs Donald
was the only person in the building with the curious thrifty practice
of washing cinders.

Helen's blood was group O. Small bloodstains of this group
were found in the Donalds' flat on a packet of soapflakes, a
scrubbing brush and a washing-up cloth. Moreover the blood on
the cloth showed traces of intestinal bacteria identical to that
found in the blood around Helen's internal injuries. It looked as
though some one had carefully cleaned up the Donalds' kitchen to
remove all traces of an assault on Helen, but had then not thought
to clean the cleaning things themselves. One or both of the
Donalds appeared to be a murderer of some cunning. Both were
arrested.

Alexander was quickly released. It was established beyond
question that he had indeed been quite normally and properly at
work in the hairdressing salon throughout the child's dinner hour
and well into the time when the search for her had started.

Jeannie's claim to have been shopping between 1.00 p.m. and
2.15 collapsed under investigation, however. She had been very
circumstantial in citing prices of groceries she had bought and
describing fabrics she had examined in a shop. It proved that her
prices were a week out of date, and the fabrics she itemized had
been sold out before 20 April.

Less conclusive, but more interesting in exonerating Alexander
and possibly incriminating Jeannie, was the fact that the child had
*not* been raped. The *post mortem* revealed no traces of semen, and
showed that the child's injuries had been caused by something
quite different from a human organ. In fact she had been assaulted
with a strong rigid instrument like a poker or the stick Scottish

housewives use for stirring porridge. What on earth had Mrs Donald been up to?

No one imagined at the time or has ever suggested since that Jeannie Donald deliberately tortured the child with an obscene and brutal assault. It has always been felt that she was trying to disguise her own involvement in Helen's death by leaving a clue that would positively indicate a male murderer. Indeed, it was once thought that she wanted Alexander to be blamed. But it was very puzzling that the phoney 'rape' had been committed *before* the child was strangled.

The *post mortem* produced another piece of evidence about Helen's physique which permitted a plausible speculation to explain this mystery. Helen suffered from an overgrowth of lymphatic tissue. This would make her unusually prone to fainting. Suppose, the prosecutors speculated, she had infuriated Mrs Donald by one of her usual childish tricks on the way out – playing 'knick-knock', or shouting, 'Coconut!' as she passed the door. Suppose, this time, Mrs Donald had been waiting for her; had caught her in the passage and given her a good shaking. And suppose the child then went into a dead faint. Might Jeannie Donald have thought Helen had died, and decided to disguise this accidental homicide as the work of a rapist, only to have the child come round as she was faking the rape? Might the strangulation itself have been a sheer accident as a frightened Jeannie struggled to silence the child's screams? A slater who had been walking to work had already told the police that he did hear a scream 'like a frightened child' come from the building around 2.00 p.m. on 20 April.

It is interesting that this hypothetical reconstruction of events came from the police and the prosecution and not from the defence. They were sufficiently convinced that they had grasped the course of the killing correctly that they invited Mrs Donald to plead guilty to manslaughter rather than face a charge of murder. But Mrs Donald and her legal advisers thought the major charge would fall when presented to a jury, and she went ahead with a plea of not guilty to murder. This failed, and after a mere quarter-hour's deliberation, the jury found her guilty.

The death sentence was commuted to life imprisonment. And evidently, both the authorities and Alexander discounted the suggestion that the faked rape was intended to implicate him. For after Jeannie had been in prison for ten years he fell terminally ill, and she was granted compassionate parole to care for him. He died shortly afterwards, and it was decided that Jeannie should be allowed to remain at liberty. She lived blamelessly under a new identity in another part of Scotland thereafter, keeping to herself the detailed events of that dreadful afternoon of 20 April 1934.

# 4

# Diane Downs

On 19 May 1983 doctors and nurses in the emergency room of McKenzie-Willamette Hospital, Springfield, Oregon, worked desperately to save the lives of two children with gunshot wounds in the chest. A third was dead on arrival. Their mother was less seriously injured: shot through the left arm.

Eight-year-old Christie Downs was clinically dead when she reached the emergency room. Doctors revived her heart and ensured that she had a chance of living, though they still did not know whether she might not suffer lasting brain damage. In the event, a stroke left her with slight speech difficulties and one paralysed arm, but no loss of intelligence or memory.

Three-year-old Danny was not so close to death as his sister. Yet he, too, was only saved by intense and dedicated medical work. His lasting injuries were to be worse: permanent paralysis from the chest down.

Seven-year-old Cheryl could not be revived.

Throughout the urgent struggle to save the children, doctors and nurses had little time to notice the mother's unusual behaviour. Afterwards it struck them rather forcefully.

Police, too, found their sympathy dissolving as the striking young blonde woman with a perfect figure displayed startlingly little interest in her children's fate. Observers could accept Diane Downs' tearlessness and taut self-control as shock, though it was unaccompanied by the normal expression of disbelief at the violent events which had overtaken her and her family. They could not understand her obsessive conversation about her boy friend in Arizona at a time when her children's lives hung by a thread. And one doctor was especially chilled when Diane told him she *knew* Christie was brain-damaged, and asked him *not* to save her life. Dr Wilhite had never ever heard a *mother* make such a request.

Diane told a story which seemed all too plausible in these sad days when rootless youth can lose itself in drug-dealing and mindless violence. She had taken her children out in the evening as she went to visit her friend Heather Plourd. The children had patted Heather's horse while Diane and Heather talked, and then, for a treat, Diane decided to take the kids for a drive looking at the country. The family had only recently moved to Oregon from Arizona, and although night had fallen, sightseeing still had its attractions.

On a dark stretch of lonely Old Mohawk Road, they passed a parked yellow car, and then, directly in the path of their own car, a man loomed up, signalling them urgently to stop. Diane got out and asked him what was wrong. He said he wanted her car. She was astonished by this request, and then horrified when he leaned in through the driving window and shot her children. She pretended to throw the car keys into the bushes. This distracted him: he turned to her and fired two more shots, one of which hit her left arm.

Diane kicked him, pushed him aside, leapt into the car, wrapped a beach towel round her injured arm, and drove pell-mell for the hospital, where she collapsed over the horn until help arrived.

Detectives quickly went to the lonely road area, looking for the old yellow car Diane had seen, and the unshaven, shaggy-haired young white male in jeans and a denim jacket who had committed this horrible unprovoked crime. The area was quiet and peaceful. The murderer had apparently escaped without disturbing any nearby residents or livestock.

Diane's peculiar manner proved to be a normal part of her personality. She was habitually a motor-mouth; talking non-stop, and smiling quite inappropriately to mask distress or tension.

But a couple of points came to worry detectives seriously. The description of a wild-haired unshaven stranger committing a violent crime is almost invariably put forward by people who . . . well . . . turn out to have been the criminals themselves. A clean shot through the left forearm passing from the palm side to the back-of-hand side is the almost invariable wound right-handed people will inflict on themselves if they want to couple maximum evidence of having been attacked with minimum long-term damage. And could anyone really accept that a mother, seeing her children fired upon by a stranger, would . . . pretend to throw her car keys into the bushes? Wouldn't almost all mothers rush forward and attack the man regardless of danger to themselves? Wouldn't any who refrained actually be quite immobilized by shock and horror? Diane quickly became the prime suspect.

Investigation of her life suggested that she had never been a perfect parent. Her three children spent their lives being shunted out to baby-sitters. And Diane admitted to screaming at them and hitting them whenever she was herself under stress.

She was a very unstable personality, with narcissistic, histrionic and sociopathic disorders. In plain English, she was unrealistically obsessed with herself; inclined to turn her life into overdramatized play-acting; and had no conscience to inform her of other people's needs. She had been brought up in a strict Baptist family, and feared her father. She claimed to have been molested by him when she was twelve. She was highly intelligent and relatively under-educated. She had unrealistic ambitions to become a doctor, and had only made it to being a postwoman. After an early unhappy marriage, she had become a surrogate mother, relishing the attention and limited publicity she gained when she proposed setting up her own surrogate mothers' agency in Arizona. She also became highly promiscuous, with a strong preference for married lovers. In 1982 she had started a passionate affair with fellow-postman Lew Lewiston, but failed to break up his marriage. Lew was drawn, but said he had no wish to be a father. Diane's children were an obstacle to her winning Lew, whose name she had tattooed on her back beneath a perfect rose.

Diane's move from Oregon to Arizona had been a partial attempt to resolve this tangle (and partially a characteristic running away from unhappiness). She telephoned Lew daily, and hoped he would leave his wife and join her. Instead, he took to refusing her calls, until the tragic day when he was told that Cheryl had been killed, and Christie and Danny lay shot.

Prima facie, there was evidence to support Diane's story. Her hand, tested chemically when she entered hospital with her injured children, bore no marks of having fired a gun. The suggestion that a woman would try to kill her children merely to get them out of the way of an unwilling lover seemed unlikely (though Louise Masset

killed her son in 1902 with exactly this motive). How could Diane
be so incompetent as to fail to kill at point-blank range? The
murder weapon was never found – so how could she have disposed
of it?

The State's answer was that she had stopped a little way along
Old Mohawk Road from the murder spot, at a point where the
river ran closest to the highway. There she had shot herself;
wrapped her arm in the perfectly prepared triangular bandage she
had made of the beach towel; and thrown the gun into the water.
Shell-casings had been found at that point, and another motorist
had seen her driving away at a snail's pace: not burning her tyres
for the hospital as she claimed.

Christie and Danny were months in intensive care. Before they
were released from hospital the State had decided Diane was not a
fit person to have care and control of them. They were removed
from her custody, and, at length, she was denied access to them.
This apparently heartless treatment of an injured and bereaved
mother made her a sympathetic celebrity in the American north-
west, and she revelled in her emotional television appearances.

It required further months of rest and therapy before Christie
could remember and recount the events of the murder night.
Danny had been asleep when he was shot, and never produced
much more than infant fantasy about 'a long-eared monster'.

But Christie had been awake and did at last remember. First she
drew what had happened. Then she mimed it. The she wrote the
name of Cheryl's killer in a sealed envelope. And finally she said it
out loud. Mom killed Cheryl. Mom shot Christie and Danny.
When she said that in court, it was the end of Diane Downs' dream
of freedom and sympathy. She was sentenced to life plus fifty years,
by a judge who expressed the hope that she would never be freed.
Christie and Danny have been happily adopted, and are leaving
behind the terrible trauma of 19 May 1983.

# 5

## Constance Kent

Here's a mystery which still puzzles crime historians after 128 years.

On 30 June 1860, the family at Road-Hill House near Trowbridge in Wiltshire was alarmed on awakening to find that little Francis Savile Kent was missing. Elizabeth Gough, the nurse, said that she had woken at 5.00 a.m. to find the child's cot empty. She assumed, she claimed, that the boy had been restless during the night, and his mother had taken him into her bed without disturbing her.

Mrs Kent strongly denied this. She called the nursemaid a wicked girl, and insisted that she had always said she was to be called immediately if there was anything amiss with her three-and-a-half-year-old son. (Later she would deny this.)

Paterfamilias Mr Samuel Kent lay unmoved in his bed through all the pother. He was not, his wife remarked, asleep. But his eyes were closed.

Two of the missing child's half-sisters came down from the upper floor where they slept among the servants' bedrooms. They expressed great distress at the disappearance of their little brother. Constance, the third, then sixteen came down too. But she stood wide-eyed and silent, making no more comment than her father.

From downstairs, the servants reported that a dining-room window and shutter had been opened during the night. This desecration of his nightly locking-up roused Mr Kent into action.

Ordering a search to be made, he took out his pony and trap, and set off for Trowbridge, five miles away, to summon the police.

While he was away, two labourers who had joined in the search of the grounds discovered young Savile. His body had been thrust behind the splashboard of the outside privy in the grounds of Road-Hill House. His throat had been cut from ear to ear and there was a deep stab wound between his ribs.

Mr Kent was a factory inspector: a man of some standing, and he effectively overruled the police and directed the immediate conduct of the case.

He had the outside of the house and the grounds searched thoroughly. He suggested that angry cottagers whose fishing rights he had suspended might have sought revenge. Or gypsies might have stolen the child. He was most unwilling to admit the possibility that anyone in the house might be responsible, although that conclusion was steadily growing on the police.

But still they respected Mr Kent's authority. A search of the persons and clothing of the Road-Hill House occupants was restricted to the servants. A policeman found an old bloodstained shift – a coarse petticoat that might be worn as either an undergarment or a nightgown – wrapped in paper and stuffed in the back of the scullery boiler. It was obviously a servant's, but the police watch on the kitchen and scullery was sufficiently impeded that its owner managed to recover it secretly.

It was not the only missing garment of its kind. When Mrs Holly the village laundress opened the Road-Hill House laundry basket and checked the washing on the day of the crime, there were two nightdresses and not the listed three enclosed. Constance's was missing.

After two fruitless weeks, Inspector Jonathan Whicher came down from Scotland Yard and latched on to the missing nightgown as a clue. Constance was an obviously disturbed adolescent: a naughty girl whose stepmother had to punish her repeatedly. She was bold and defiant. In 1856 she had run away from home disguised as a boy, intending to go to Bristol and take ship as a cabin boy for the West Indies. She had cut off her long hair and thrown it down the privy where Savile's body was found four years later. The police called her a little heroine.

A spirited young girl; an indomitable young girl; and one profoundly alienated from her family.

Mr and Mrs Kent were deeply unloveable examples of the

good Victorian husband and wife: family prayers every day; holy wedlock until death did them part; a righteous insistence that inferiors and children know their place and learn their duty; and withal, a heavy dose of nauseating humbug.

While Constance's mother, Mr Kent's first wife, was alive, Elizabeth Pratt had been the children's nurse and governess. And their father's mistress. She was twenty years younger than the first Mrs Kent. Twenty years prettier and more ambitious. The other servants were ordered to treat her as family. Mrs Kent was pushed into back rooms and ignored. Elizabeth Pratt ruled the roost.

Mr Kent had to move three times to escape the local gossip this caused. Also because he kept running out of servants willing to work for him, since he was mean with wages and parsimonious with food.

He had to be. For his houses and life-style were beyond his perfectly adequate means. Financial worries made promotion in the Inspectorate important for him. Constance's runaway escapade didn't do his character any good.

As Elizabeth gained power in the household, she wickedly strove to turn Mrs Kent's children against her; to persuade them that their mother was useless, unimportant, unloveable. Little Constance came to believe this at first, and loved her nurse. But when Mrs Kent died, Mr Kent and Elizabeth married, and Constance and her sisters were displaced by the new family. The new Mrs Kent was a typical wicked stepmother.

Inspector Whicher learned from Mr Kent that his first wife had been mentally unstable: that there was a good deal of madness in her family. Without directly saying so, Mr Kent hinted that this might have come out in Constance. Inspector Whicher acted decisively, if precipitately. He arrested Constance, and she was charged with murdering her little brother.

An effective and emotional Victorian barrister blew the case to smithereens. Constance had been romping happily with the child the afternoon before he died. She had no motive, and almost certainly not the strength to carry the dead weight of a 35 lb toddler through the house and out to the privy without waking the household. She was discharged on a strong tide of local sympathy.

To other people, Mr Kent looked far more like the guilty party. His actions on 30 June suggested that he wanted to be out of the way when the body was found. When the police arrived he had

hampered them in their search and refused to let them examine the
whole of his house.

Gossip turned on his behaviour during his first marriage. Had
he repeated the pattern? Had Elizabeth Gough, the new nursemaid, become his new mistress? Had the notoriously talkative little
Savile woken up to see the two in a compromising position in the
nursery? Had Mr Kent – deliberately or accidentally – suffocated
his son in silencing him, and then cut his throat and stabbed him to
make him look like the victim of an outsider? For medical evidence
now suggested that the child had indeed been suffocated first, and
only then, and quite unnecessarily suffered the knife wounds.
Whose was the woman's chest-cloth without strings – a sort of
primitive brassière – found in the privy under the body? Why was
Savile's cot carefully remade to look undisturbed, even though a
blanket had been removed to wrap the body in, and the mattress
and pillow showed unnaturally deep impressions of his head and
thigh, as though someone had held him down and smothered him
where he lay?

The police charged Elizabeth Gough with the murder, hoping
Mr Kent's implication might emerge. This charge failed, too, and
the case lay a mystery for five years.

Constance was sent to France to complete her education, and on
reaching her majority in 1865 took her small inheritance from her
mother, and went to St Mary's Anglican Convent in Brighton to
train as a nurse. The fervid Anglo-Catholicism of the place gripped
her. She arranged to be confirmed by the Reverend Mr Wagner,
the institution's spiritual director, and admitted to him, both in
and out of the confessional, that she had killed Savile.

Mr Wagner persuaded her to repeat the confession to the police
in London, and despite all encouragement to offer a defence, she
insisted on going to trial and pleading guilty. Her inevitable death
sentence was commuted to life imprisonment. She served twenty
years; was released; and disappeared.

She went to Australia under a new name and completed her
nursing training, thereafter leading a happy, jolly and useful life.
When a book on her trial came out, an anonymous letter from
Sydney gave the author new and detailed inside information about
Constance's childhood, and defended the first Mrs Kent against
the charge of insanity. It was not from Constance, but from
someone close to her who made the error Constance could never
have made of thinking she had precociously called Sarah

Bernhardt 'the Divine Sarah' while still a schoolgirl. Sarah Bernhardt never appeared on stage until Constance was in prison.

On her hundredth birthday in 1944 'Miss Emily Kaye' became the only convicted murderess ever to receive the royal telegram of congratulations. She had successfully put the case behind her. So why don't we?

We don't because we can't. Her confession didn't and doesn't make sense. Constance claimed to have used one of her father's razors to cut Savile's throat and inflict the stab wound accidentally as she tried to push the body further into the privy. This is a completely impossible lie. A cut-throat razor simply could not have inflicted the wound between the ribs. She claimed to have stuffed her old chest-cloth into his mouth, and carried him silently through the house and out of the window (putting on galoshes on the way). This seems practically impossible. She said that her motive was to avenge her mother's memory and – she didn't put it quite like this – to assuage her own guilt for having ever preferred her stepmother, by destroying the child her stepmother loved, just as her stepmother had destroyed the first Mrs Kent's happiness in Constance's love. This seems possible, but far-fetched, and quite uncharacteristic of the determined, positive, constructive and admirable woman she became.

So who did kill Savile Kent? Three possibilities have been mooted. Constance herself, much as she confessed, though for some unknown reason she put forward untrue details in her confession. Or Mr Kent, with or without the help, though pretty certainly with the knowledge, of Elizabeth Gough. Constance, in this case, becomes, in Yseult Bridges' words, a 'Saint with red hands,' deliberately lifting the scandal and suspicion from her father by falsely accepting all the guilt herself. This, of course, makes Mr Kent a truly appalling villain, deliberately trying to save his own skin by casting suspicion on his blameless daughter, and hiding behind her skirts when she high-mindedly set out to save him.

Finally there is Bernard Taylor's recent suggestion. Constance killed Savile by suffocation. Mr Kent carried out the subsequent disposal of the body and the throat-cutting and stabbing to disguise his daughter's action, and did his best to save her life by holding up the police enquiry, and inventing the mental disturbance of his first wife to try and help Constance cheat the gallows, should she be charged.

All accounts agree that religious hysteria prompted Constance's confession, and it must be seen as more or less unreliable. But if it was mere juvenile heroics, why did she stick to it through twenty wretched years of prison, abused by staff and prisoners alike as a child-murderer? If it was substantially true, why did newly converted Christian Constance include blatant lies about the razor?

It's an intriguing mystery, isn't it? Who do you think killed Savile Kent?

# Part three
# FATAL FALSE GLAMOUR

# 1

# William Desmond Taylor

Hollywood Babylon! Glamour, glitter and greed! Drink, drugs and dear little girlies! Bootleggers, bimbos and bullets! Assignations, adultery and assassinations! Death wrapped in tinsel. The murder of William Desmond Taylor.

You remember the story and the mystery? Henry Peavey, Taylor's black manservant, found the elegant English director dead on the floor of his Hollywood home early one morning in 1922. An upright chair had fallen over his legs. A strange monogrammed handkerchief lay by the body, and the ashtray suggested that someone else had been in the room when or shortly before Taylor died. But there was nothing obvious to suggest foul play. A passing doctor who made the first diagnosis simply put death down to haemorrhage from an ulcerated stomach, and went on his way.

The police, when they arrived, found the house full of studio heads, anxiously removing compromising papers and bottles of booze. They also found film star Mabel Normand frantically going through drawers in the bedroom searching for her private letters.

The police uncovered some shocking private material. An envelope full of pornographic photographs showing Taylor with many film stars, including Mabel Normand. A collection of silk panties, all marked by the trophy-hunting Taylor with the dates of the conquests they represented. A silk nightdress with the monogram MMM, pointing unerringly to Mary Miles Minter, Mary Pickford's new rival as a little innocent under-age sweetheart for America. Love letters from Mary Miles Minter showing that she was anything but innocent.

The police also turned the body over and found what the transient doctor had missed. A bullet hole in Taylor's back.

Further enquiries revealed further mystery. Mabel Normand had visited Taylor the previous night, bringing a large bag of peanuts. Shortly after the shooting (heard by neighbours at midnight, but put down to the backfiring of a passing car) a strange figure was seen walking away from Taylor's house. A man in cap and muffler? Or a woman disguised as a man? Or just a woman? Accounts varied. Could it have been Mabel Normand? Disguised as a man?

And was Taylor being blackmailed? He had withdrawn a large sum of money from his bank account just before he died. That bank account was strangely small for a highly paid director.

He was certainly a man of mystery. He was really William Deane Tanner, a successful antiques dealer in New York, who had suddenly deserted his wife; disappeared for a few years, during which he was seen working in various humble occupations in different parts of the country, until he turned up in Hollywood and rose rapidly from modestly successful actor to extremely successful director.

And he had a brother, Dennis Deane Tanner, who had also deserted his American wife and disappeared. Was Dennis Deane Tanner in fact the mysterious valet Edward Sands, Henry Peavey's predecessor, who had robbed Taylor and absconded with his chequebook, leaving a trail of forged cheques, in spite of which, the police and Taylor between them had failed to bring him to book? Did Taylor deliberately spare Sands because he loved him as his ne'er-do-well brother? Or – a darker whisper – had Sands been his homosexual lover? Was it significant that Henry Peavey was shortly to face a morals charge for picking up young boys in the park?

The notion of Taylor as a homosexual was rapidly dismissed in view of the hoard of panties and porno-pix.

Police enquiries uncovered a lot of dirt, but no murderer. Mabel Normand was under strong suspicion. Had her affair with Taylor been brought to a sudden end by his new passion for Mary Miles Minter? Was it a jealousy killing? Thorough investigation failed to produce evidence against her.

What about little Mary Miles Minter herself? The naïve little actress had claimed to be engaged to Taylor. One of her notes to him, on pretty butterfly-headed writing-paper said little more than, 'I love you – I love you – I love you,' followed by twenty kisses. Did the discovery of Taylor's promiscuous life-style or his ongoing relationship with Mabel Normand drive her to distraction and lead her to shoot a lover who refused to stop collecting panties and their contents? Thorough-going detective work failed to result in any charges being brought.

All right, so what about Mary Miles Minter's mother? The former actress Charlotte Shelby, she was the stage mother to end all stage mothers. She kept a tenacious grip on all Mary's earnings, managing her and dishing out a mere sufficiency of pocket money. She followed her around the studios at work, jealously ensuring that her little meal-ticket never compromised the profitable innocence that made her such a bankable film heroine. She made her daughter go to bed early and alone. She had a fortune riding on the girl's uncorrupted reputation, and she wouldn't take kindly to her falling into the hands of a suave English satyr.

Alas, the entire family of Mary Miles Minter had an unshake-able alibi. Mary, her undoubtedly innocent sister Margaret, and their mother had all been peacefully at home on the night Taylor was killed, and Mary had been reading to them from *Tales of the South Seas*. These were the days before radio, and such quiet self-provided home entertainment was perfectly normal.

The whole enquiry ground to a halt. No murderer was discovered. No charges were brought.

But Mary Miles Minter's career stopped dead in its tracks. Mabel Normand's hiccupped wildly; then ran down; and she committed suicide. The scandal and the mystery were virtually forgotten until the 1960s saw the decay of the film industry and revived interest in its early history and golden era.

Then, in 1967, the ageing director King Vidor recalled the William Desmond Taylor affair and saw in it the making of a successful film about early Hollywood. He set up a production company and started to investigate all that nearly-forgotten material. Somewhat to his surprise, he discovered that the file was still open, and Los Angeles still employed police detectives who would be only too happy to have the case solved and closed. And although they were pretty tight-lipped, it seemed they had little doubt a solution could be found. At least to the satisfaction of historians.

Courts and District Attorneys were another matter. The
physical evidence – the *proof* needed – no longer existed. And
successive District Attorneys had taken over-enthusiastic
detectives off the case as soon as they approached certainty that
they knew who had done it, but seemed to be contemplating arrests
and charges that would break down when the case came to court.

By the end of 1967 Vidor knew who had done it. He also knew he
could never make a film of it. And he sealed his findings in a
strongbox, unable and unwilling to publish them while they might
still hurt the living.

By 1986 Vidor himself was dead, and the writer Sidney
Kirkpatrick went to work on his life. He found the strongbox;
investigated Vidor's findings; and published, at long last, the
solution to the 64-year-old mystery instead of the biography he had
intended.

Vidor and Kirkpatrick's first and most remarkable discovery
was that a good deal of the familiar material of the scandal was
sheer fiction, discreetly peddled by studio press offices for somewhat nefarious purposes. Los Angeles Police Department knew
this perfectly well, and was quite content to let the newspapers
headline rubbish, while the detectives quietly went on pursuing
the real culprit behind the smokescreen.

Vidor was amazed to find that William Desmond Taylor's
notorious sex-life was a complete invention. There were no porno-
pix of himself in action: there was no collection of date-stamped
panties. Mabel Normand had never tried to recover her compromising letters, for there were none. There had been a nightdress
embroidered MMM, but the police ignored it as it might easily
have been placed there by studio heads to mislead them.

For the studio heads were particularly anxious to cover up one
genuine scandal. Taylor had been homosexual. Henry Peavey's
excursions to the park had not been for his own satisfaction; they
had been to procure boys for his employer. Mary Miles Minter had
thrown herself passionately at the svelte director who led her to
stardom, but found her advances coolly and definitely resisted.
Mabel Normand was, in an unusually accurate sense of the words,
just a good friend.

This lacked the general tawdry glamour of heterosexual
promiscuity, and might even start a witch-hunt for other homo-
sexuals in Hollywood. It could not be turned to the studios'
advantage.

Heterosexual scandals, on the other hand, could. Astonishingly, the studio bosses were only too pleased to have Mabel Normand and Mary Miles Minter publicly excoriated for immorality. Studio-created stars sometimes became monsters. Since their publicity-hyped personalities ensured that audiences flocked to their pictures all over the world, they were a major financial investment. Their appearance could guarantee the success of their pictures. And knowing their strength, they demanded more and more money, and behaved worse and worse when they were working. Mabel's drug-addiction had made her unpredictable and unreliable. The studios actually wanted her to fall from grace with the public.

Mary Miles Minter was an even less desirable property. Her last five films had flopped. Only her mother's overweening ambition kept her going as an actress: she had lost interest, and it showed. The studio would be well served by a scandal which entitled them to terminate her contract.

None the less, the secret of Taylor's killing did not lie in the homosexual world. The police found out very quickly that the cheque-bouncing Edward Sands and Dennis Deane Tanner were completely different people, and Sands's disappearance was caused by his death in New England.

Nor was Taylor being blackmailed. His empty bank account was one of three: the others were full. His large withdrawal had been for a quite legitimate business speculation.

No, Mary Miles Minter *was* in fact involved. Police had found three blonde hairs matching hers on the jacket Taylor was wearing when he was shot. And they linked the bullet that shot him with a gun owned by Charlotte Shelby. What happened, and how was it covered up?

Vidor and Kirkpatrick found more evidence on police files, and in the almost confessional testimony in a number of financial lawsuits Mary and her mother brought against each other. They reconstructed the killing thus. On the day of Taylor's death, Charlotte Shelby was making furious attempts to find out whether the director was debauching her daughter, or intended to marry her and steal mamma's little meal-ticket. And, in fact, Mary was pursuing the director hard, if hopelessly.

During the evening, Mary went to Taylor's house to pester him, and was there when Mabel Normand innocently dropped in. Mary promptly hid upstairs and waited for Mabel to leave.

While Mabel and Taylor were talking Charlotte Shelby arrived with her gun, intending to threaten Taylor if he would not leave Mary alone. She waited outside the back door, smoking cigarettes, until Mabel left. Then she walked in. As she did so, Mary came down the stairs.

This, for the termagant Charlotte, was proof that she had been deceived. In a rage, she shot Taylor and left through the front door. With her flat cap-like hat and muffler, hers was the 'man's' figure seen by one neighbour, who didn't catch sight of her legs. The woman seen by another might have been Mabel leaving just before the shooting, or Mary leaving just after.

The Shelby family alibi was, of course, concocted. Innocent Margaret, with nothing to hide personally, could not even remember accurately the book title Mary was supposed to have been reading in the peaceful domestic scene.

But why were no charges ever brought, if so much could be demonstrated forty years later? Here was the most remarkable discovery of all. Charlotte Shelby hung on grimly to Mary Miles Minter's money. She needed it, she explained, to protect Mary's and her reputations. And in fact she used it to pay off three successive District Attorneys. They saw to it that detectives were taken off the case as soon as they approached the truth. They saw to the destruction of the all-important physical evidence: the gun, the bullet, the three blonde hairs. They kept the case open. And preserved a public mystery for sixty years.

# 2

## Libby Holman

There was a young millionaire. A pioneer aviator with a grand mansion in North Carolina and a nationally famous wife. She was a sexy torch singer, whose throaty voice captivated millions. A star of the bedroom whose wide selection of male and female lovers made her a constant figure in the gossip columns.

This fashionable couple gave a wild party during prohibition: a few friends and a lot of hooch. The sexy wife and a girl friend got very smashed and sort of danced on tables. The millionaire husband was a bit embarrassed. More embarrassed still when he found his wife kissing his best friend in the shrubbery. Embarrassed again when she disappeared for three hours and could not be found in the mansion or its grounds. But then, it was the sort of party where the wife's smashed friend went off with a cute young southern gentleman in his motor car for a drive, and stayed away for a couple of hours. And then went to bed. Hearing almost nothing of the night's future events.

The night's events included the return of the sexy wife; the removal of her fashionable lounging pyjamas in the mansion's grand living-room, in the presence of the husband, and his best friend, and the cute young southern gentleman; the removal of the sexy wife to her bedroom, where a very loud quarrel took place between husband and wife; the departure from the house of the southern gentleman (an interval in which the precise whereabouts of the husband, the wife and the husband's best friend become uncertain); and a muffled shot. Then came screams and cries from

the wife, disturbing her sleeping girl friend, and a sudden apparent
realization by the husband's best friend that something was amiss.
The young millionaire was discovered shot through the head on
the balcony of his luxurious bedroom. There were ambiguous signs
at the entry wound – was it or wasn't it fired close enough to be
suicide? The doctors disagreed.

It sounds more like a novel by Margery Allingham than a piece
of history, don't you agree? A cast of fiction-worthy characters in
an improbably glamorous setting. A mystery that has never been
solved. And a sinister aura left over the remainder of the torch
singer's career.

Dragging it back to reality is just a matter of dotting the 'i's and
crossing the 't's. The characters don't actually change. But
brought into focus, they come down to earth with a bump.

Smith Reynolds was one of the heirs to the massive fortune built
around Camel cigarettes and the Winston-Salem tobacco enterprises. As a pioneer aviator he never made it around the world. His
planes kept breaking down. And at heart, he was a very ordinary,
gauche country boy who happened to have enough money to carry
his humdrum enthusiasms wherever he liked. When he fell in love
with Libby Holman, he took front seats at all her concerts; tagged
himself on to all her after-show parties; evoked the amused
contempt of her witty, cosmopolitan, homosexual show-biz
friends; and only raised the world's eyebrows when the sophisticated Libby married this boy who had been brandishing his calf-
love at her for years.

And Libby herself? Well, she wasn't a very good singer. It was
quite late in her career before she could hold her pitch securely.
She didn't have outstanding taste or a perfect style of delivery. Just
a rich throaty voice and an admiration for Bessie Smith. And the
extremely good luck to make an early friend of the totally
disciplined, totally professional actor-dancer-comedian Clifton
Webb.

She worked with him in his long-time dream of doing a
sung-and-danced sketch about a pimp and a whore that should
make the Apache dance look like a Sunday School recitation. She
was given her first great hit song, 'Moanin' Low' for the purpose.
Her second great hit, 'Body and Soul' was written for another show
done with Webb. And she had the sensual presence to make those
songs unforgettable when she belted them.

It was presence, mind you, not genuine sensuality. She wasn't beautiful. Her pudgy face had hamster cheeks, and her extremely myopic eyes tended to squint. Her hair was a coarse mop unless it had been recently teased into a fashionable bob. Her skin was a dull olive, although this could seem like exotic mulatto under stage conditions.

And her come-hither vampish manner, as remarkable numbers of kiss-and-tell lovers have survived to report, faded badly when she got into bed. Libby Holman initiated more seductions than she could count. She competed recklessly with her friend Tallulah Bankhead for the reputation of making it with any he, she or it that could make it. She talked so dirty that Dorothy Parker told her she ought to wear her knickers over her face. But she didn't enjoy sex.

It was the boring price that had to be paid for the excitement of exerting seductive power over men or women. Oh, she paid it properly enough. She wasn't a selfish tease. But she never ever came herself. She tolerated other people enjoying her body. And she turned savagely bitchy, reading it as rejection, if they failed.

Smith Reynolds had started to fail. In the solitude of his home he played threateningly with a pistol and talked increasingly about suicide. His public gaucheness was starting to accompany private impotence. Five years younger than his dominating wife, he had not persuaded her that a woman's place was in the home; a millionaire hubby would be the bread-winner, and wifey should be a domestic ornament to be admired by his provincial friends.

Those friends were dreary hicks, to Libby. Dull Carolina Tarheels. The only interest they shared with her jazzy New York friends was getting drunk. But in New York this important cultural activity was carried out in glittering speakeasies to a background of urbane and suggestive malice and wit. In Winston-Salem you jest fetched a coupla barrels o' cornmash from the bootlegger in back o' the garage, took 'em home, an' asked your friends round to drink 'em all up an' git smashed.

And that's what happened on 4 July 1932. Smith invited round the richest bachelor in Winston, playboy C. G. Hill. Hill brought Virginia Dunklee, daughter of the town's largest launderer. Jim Shepherd who kept the Winston art shop came with his girl friend, Babe Vaught. Ab Walker, Smith's best friend, and nominally his secretary, was there as a fixture. So was Blanche Yurka, a Czech actress whom Libby had imported from New York to give the hick town some sense of sophistication. Three more men friends of Smith's completed the party.

Who can blame Libby and Babe for getting drunk together at
this unbalanced occasion? Who could wonder that Libby kissed
Ab when she met him down by the swimming pool? Who could be
surprised that the hopelessly drunk little lady played one of her
favourite party tricks, stripping off all her clothes to reveal a truly
beautiful body?

Of course, the hicks couldn't take it as coolly as her New York
friends. A marital quarrel followed.

And then? Libby was genuinely too drunk to know what
happened. Ab Walker was desperately covering up something.
Possibly connected with his possession of Smith's empty wallet
after his death, which he said Smith had tossed to him because it
contained his final wages. Possibly connected with a suspicion on
his part that Libby had shot her husband in a drunken quarrel.
Possibly connected with a fear that his dilatory procedures after
what he believed to be a minor gun accident had led to his friend's
unnecessary death.

But certainly not, as malicious gossip asserted, a calculated
murder arranged between him and Libby because they had
become lovers; because the child she was carrying was Ab's and
both wanted to be rid of the man who was Ab's homosexual lover
as well as her husband. Although this scandalous and fictitious
scenario led to murder charges being brought against both of
them, it is almost certain that Smith's hair-trigger pistol went off
accidentally during a quarrel in which he had once again
threatened suicide. It was probably in Libby's drunken hands at
the time, and Ab was probably trying to cover up what he knew to
have been a tragic accident.

More tragically still, the whole truth was never brought out in
court. The powerful Reynolds family forced the dropping of the
prosecution, more to silence gossip than from a genuine conviction
of Libby's innocence. And the poor woman went through the
remainder of a long and ultimately very useful life, giving
considerable sums of money to scientific education and the peace
movement and Martin Luther King's good causes, never sure
whether or why she might have killed her husband while smashed
out of her mind.

The study of murder has given me more sympathy with
teetotalism than I would ever have believed possible.

# 3

# Rudolf Lorenz

The island of Floreana in the Galapagos archipelago was the scene of weird and wonderful happenings in the 1930s. Its strange colony of German escapists and eccentrics attracted a good deal of attention in the international press. The two most sensational households broke up in chaos and disaster with two disappearances and two deaths. And then world affairs and the war led to their all being forgotten.

Admirers of the philosopher Nietzsche are in danger of adopting some rather dubious attitudes. His notion of a group of Supermen whose manifest superiority to everyone else entitles them to ride roughshod over the rest of the world is not one that can be safely adopted. It's likely to be pretty bad for the soul to consider yourself intrinsically better than the rest of mankind. Like the Nietzschean *übermennschen* of the Nazi party you may well wind up being quite correctly perceived as manifestly inferior to the dullest and most ordinary of people.

Dr Friedrich Ritter was, in his own esteem, a Superman. His mistress Dore Strauch agreed that he was one of the great thinkers of the twentieth century (though no publisher has yet found his philosophical ramblings commercially or academically viable.) Dore was prepared to devote her life to serving this lofty giant among men.

To the rest of us, he looks more like a selfish, boorish, bullying crank: a wife-beater (well, Nietzseheans know that the master said, 'Are you going to the woman? Do not forget your whip.'); a vegetarian (unless meat proved too tempting); a dietary faddist who believed that flour was unhealthy and half the ills of modern civilization came from eating bread and cake, who thought that coffee was toxic, who believed that houses built in mystical circular shapes were *scientifically* preferable to ordinary squares or oblongs, and that gardens shaped like eggs would yield better produce than any other kind; a man who felt seriously undervalued by the horrid *üntermennschen* of Germany in 1932, and sought an uninhabited island where, like Robinson Crusoe, he could be king of all he surveyed.

He left his wife; persuaded Dore Strauch to leave her husband; and made for Floreana where all previous attempts to settle had failed. Dr Ritter had no doubt that he would set new standards of solitary human achievement.

Once on the island, the cranky couple built themselves a ramshackle house with the remarkably suburban name of Friedo, for Friedrich and Dore. They laid out an egg-shaped garden. They devised ingenious refinements like a wooden press to crush sugar-cane, and a faucet made out of a shell to control the running spring water piped and troughed into one corner of their shack. And Friedrich wrote pieces for the newspapers about their idyllic Adam and Eve life in Paradise.

Strangely, he omitted to describe his utter cruelty and brutality to Dore: the serious injury inflicted on her leg during the first week in Paradise which left her limping for the rest of her life; the savage hatred which sprang up between them, covered, for public observation, by his silent and superior contempt for her as for the rest of creation. And by her masochistic acceptance of Nietzschean female inferiority at all times when she could suppress her loathing and detestation for the abominable man she had accompanied to the other end of nowhere.

The newspapers adored the idea of two nudists enjoying bliss in the tropical wilderness. Even the quaint and absurd observation that they had only one set of stainless steel false teeth, which they shared between them to compensate for the curious dental inferiority marring their superperson status, failed to detract from the notion that they had found a wonderful escape from industrial turmoil. Within a year they had been joined by another family.

Heinz Wittmer was secretary to the young Konrad Adenauer. But he was not politically-minded himself, and he and his wife Marget agreed to cash in their savings and try the Crusoe life on

Floreana. Prudently, they reserved enough money for a return to Germany in case things went wrong. They took Heinz's young son Harry with them, and without indulging in any Nietzschean nonsense, simply set up as homesteaders. They worked together amicably (whereas Friedrich had driven Dore to labour for him) and, alone among early Floreanians, succeeded in building a stone house.

The next arrivals were altogether stormier. The Baroness Wagner-Bosquet was a truly appalling woman. A 44-year-old Austrian, she had abandoned her French husband for a young curio-shop keeper in Paris. Rudolf Lorenz was infatuated by the heavy-breasted, projecting-toothed former beauty, whose manic vitality made her the centre of any crowd, and whose voracious sexuality showed him new possibilities in life. He became emotionally enslaved to her, and the Baroness enthusiastically took over running his shop; defrauded him of his profits; bankrupted him; and ordered the foolish young man to accompany her to Floreana, where she proposed to use the last of his money to open a 'Hotel Paradiso' for rich Americans. She also took with her another young German, Robert Phillipson, who was described by a visiting yachtsman as looking like a cheap gigolo picked up in a city restaurant.

The Baroness arrived in Floreana with a flourish. She brandished a pistol, and stole a large quantity of rice that had been sent for the Wittmers. She insisted on using their spring. She did not disguise the fact that both her young companions were her lovers. And she quickly designated herself 'the Empress of Floreana'.

All three households were, to a considerable extent, dependent on visiting yachts and cruise ships to bring in fresh supplies and needed hardware. An extremely attractive Californian millionaire named Allan Hancock was a particular benefactor of the Floreanians from the outset. He sailed in tropical waters with boat-guests who always included scientists, to make serious surveys of the flora and fauna, and musicians who played chamber music with him in the evenings. (He was an accomplished amateur cellist.) He made generous presents of food and goods to all the members of this strange little Germanic colony whenever he visited the Galapagos, and Superman Ritter secretly compiled begging lists of things to scrounge from Hancock and other visitors.

The Baroness was less concerned with scrounging. She simply
used her guns and her menfolk to intimidate the other settlers into
handing over anything she wanted after the visitors had left.
Hancock pleased her by having a film director shoot some footage
of her as a pirate queen, living up to an absurd story she had placed
in the newspapers about hijacking and imprisoning visiting
yachtsmen before turning them out in an open boat.

At length the Baroness's thefts and outrages grew so extreme
that Heinz Wittmer wrote a formal complaint to the Ecuadorian
governor of the Galapagos Islands. This backfired badly. The
governor came over on a visit of inspection. The Baroness took him
straight to her bed, and treated him to what she later described as
'a more than Arabian night'. The governor sailed away the next
day, having granted the Baroness four square miles of Floreana as
her own territory, while granting the other two families a mere fifty
acres apiece. The Ritters sulked furiously. The Wittmers, who had
a new baby to look after, withdrew cautiously into their shell.

All was not well, however, in the Baroness's entourage at her
so-called 'Hacienda Paradiso'. Rudolf Lorenz had been her spoilt
toy-boy when she arrived. Now she changed direction and put
Phillipson first. With the muscle of an Ecuadorian labourer at first,
and then the powerful Phillipson, backed up by the Baroness's
riding-crop, Lorenz was steadily beaten and reduced to a state of
absolute slavery. He shared his misery with the other two
households. Dore Strauch, who knew all about being beaten and
enslaved, and also had an eye for a pretty boy, was sympathetic
and concerned. Friedrich's Supermanhood did not extend to
declaring open war on a strong and ruthless woman, however. He
cursed the Baroness, and lay low.

The Wittmers, unlike their sorry crew of superior-being neighbours, did not go in for domestic violence. They were deeply
shocked by Lorenz's condition. The boy was evidently becoming
seriously ill. But they had tried once to make a proper complaint to
the responsible authorities, and the Baroness had easily routed
them by using what the West Indies would call, 'Pussy Power'.
They had their children to consider, and could do no more than
offer Lorenz shelter with them if he wanted it.

Lorenz left desperate messages in the old barrel in Post Office
Bay where, since the eighteenth century, passing yachtsmen had
deposited and picked up mail to be delivered at random as
somebody chanced to sail by in an appropriate direction. Lorenz

pleaded for anybody to come and take him off the island and rescue him. Nobody did.

Rudolf even wrote to the Baron Bosquet, begging for money for his return to Europe, and promising to supply him with evidence for a divorce from the frightful Baroness. Baron Bosquet sensibly left them all to stew in their own juice on their island hell.

In 1934, Rudolf Lorenz retreated to the Wittmers house, refusing to sleep at the Hacienda Paradiso any more. The Baroness came and visited him every day: never entering the property; always taking Lorenz off for long walks from which he returned first cheerful, then tearful.

One day the Baroness announced that she and Phillipson were off to Tahiti with a visiting English yachtsman. They looked forward to the holiday, and Lorenz was urged to stay in the Hacienda to look after their things while they were away. He departed with her, but came back later, saying that he was going to stay with the Wittmers for one more night. Marget Wittmer went down to Post Office Bay to have a look at the visiting yacht. It was nowhere to be seen. Nor was it ever heard of from any other source. There were footprints on the beach suggesting that the Baroness and Phillipson had been down there. Nothing else. The Baroness Wagner-Bosquet and Robert Phillipson were never seen again.

But this easing of tension did not result in a notably happier life for the Ritters. Dore Strauch was soon writing to Germany that she was thinking of coming home as she could stand no more of Friedrich. And Friedrich was writing to his brother suggesting that things might be patched up with his former wife as he'd had enough of Dore. It was no longer possible for them to conceal their mutual hatred from the neighbours.

Rudolf Lorenz had a bit of good luck. With the Baroness gone, and, he insisted, never to return, he sold the goods left in the Hacienda Paradiso to the Ritters and Wittmers. They were puzzled to see that the Baroness had apparently left all her personal possessions behind – family photographs, her favourite hat, and even the copy of Oscar Wilde's *The Picture of Dorian Gray* that never left her possession. But Friedrich cheerfully beat down Rudolf in the matter of prices and thought no more about it.

Rudolf used his new-found money to buy his passage off the island, and was shipwrecked together with a motor-yacht captain before they had even passed outside the archipelago. Their mummified bodies were found on a deserted island some months

later, together with their boat's skiff, after Rudolf's mysterious
disappearance had become just one more popular press talking-
point in the saga of fateful Floreana.

And then Friedrich died. He obstinately insisted that he would
eat some potted chicken meat that had long gone bad, affirming
(correctly) that however nasty, it would be perfectly safe if it were
boiled long enough. It wasn't, and he died of botulism in
considerable pain. What an irony, the cranks noted, that a
dedicated vegetarian should die of eating meat. He used his last
strength to write an evil note to Dore that read, 'With my dying
breath I curse you.'

The island was left, at last, to the quiet, ordinary loving
Wittmers, who had rejected the idea of returning to Hitler's Jew-
persecuting Germany, brought up their children in Floreana, and
founded the colony that survives there to this day.

And where does murder come into this preposterous story? In
the disappearance of the Baroness and Phillipson.

The 'missing Empress of Floreana' was noised abroad so loudly
in the sensational press that there can be little doubt that the
'English yacht going to Tahiti' never existed. John Treherne, who
discovered this odious crew in yellowing newspaper files and old
yachtsmen's memoirs, believes that the Baroness invented it as an
excuse to get her slave, Lorenz, back to the Hacienda. And he has
no doubt that Lorenz somehow found occasion to shoot his
tormentors. A sudden and a bloody end was what the self-
dramatizing Baroness and her bully-boy richly deserved. The only
question in Treherne's mind is whether Ritter helped Lorenz, and
whether Dore knew it. She threw out vague hints that her lover had
been a man of blood.

But we shall never know for sure, as in the end she had her own
cranky face to save. She returned to Germany and wrote up her
four miserable wasted years in the Galapagos as a triumph of the
soul, supporting one of the great master-minds of the twentieth
century until his tragic and accidental death.

Heigh-ho! You can't keep a bad Nietzschean down!

# 4

## Michael De Freitas

There's not much consolation in this story for anyone but a fully paid-up member of the National Front. The rest of us, if we were old enough to be politically active in the 1960s, have to ask ourselves how much we personally contributed to Gale Benson's murder.

White liberals? We were so naïve and guilt-ridden that we dared not make sensible challenges to the credentials of anyone who emerged as a black spokesman. White conservatives? They were so busy discrediting themselves by their scatter-shot attacks on the liberalization of society; so unwilling to come down clearly against apartheid as an evil, that their warnings about the criminality of Michael De Freitas went unheeded. Black radicals? They let their proper role as the spearhead of discontent be usurped by an unscrupulous self-serving charlatan. Black moderates? Their apathetic preservation of a low profile inhibited them from exposing a man they recognized as worthless. Only the out-and-out racists welcomed an aggressive and fraudulent opponent. Only they could happily crow, 'I told you so!' when the false promise of Michael De Freitas's black leadership ended in tragedy. Only they, whose attitudes and actions had done more than anything else to give the man a platform.

Michael De Freitas was born in a Port-of-Spain slum in 1933. His mother was black, his father Portuguese – a nationality which almost counts as non-white among poor Trinidadians. Michael was a 'red man', never fully accepted as resolutely black among the urban poor.

He went to a good Catholic school; got into a good deal of trouble, and was finally expelled with a half-education. He went to sea and divided his life between the West Indies and Tiger Bay, Cardiff. There he started hustling. Living off women. Pushing a little hash. If the law got close, he could take off to sea until the heat was off. It was a pattern he would follow for the remainder of his life: live dangerously on the margins of legality, and run away abroad when his criminality was about to be brought home to him.

Tiger Bay was not a good base for an ambitious young hustler with no grasp of his own limitations. Michael came to London and settled in Notting Hill. Here the serious lords of petty crime found him unimpressive. He was not very successful in turning out local girls to walk the streets for him. Not in touch with the important centres of drug trafficking. And obviously too obsessed with race; too concerned to insist that his stable should be white girls. A serious hustler wouldn't give a damn if his girls were green or purple as long as they brought home the bacon.

But in Notting Hill, Michael formed two relationships, either of which might have determined his future. If Desiree, the charming Guyanese woman he fell for and married, had controlled his destiny, it might have been relatively humble. We might not have heard of him. But he would not have died on the gallows.

Alas, West Indian men rarely let any women direct their lives. And Michael's odd racial quirk ensured that a white mentor became decisive in making him the man he became.

Peter Rachman has given his name to an evil word in the dictionary. The epitome of the bullying, rack-renting, extortionist slum landlord, Rachman may actually have been saddled with responsibility for a wide variety of sins he did not commit. For at the moment when public and government attention turned to the landlord and tenant situation in London's slums, Rachman was conveniently dead and could neither defend himself nor be libelled. Moreover, he was already notorious as a stellar figure in the early part of Mandy Rice-Davis's glorious sex-life.

Rent controls and the statutory security of tenure lent itself to certain abuses. It was one of Rachman's virtues that he willingly let accommodation to West Indians at a time when most landlords, overtly or covertly, applied the rule 'No Coloureds'. But Rachman had entered the property business by fronting for prostitutes who wanted flats. Both immigrants and prostitutes were the kind of 'undesirable' neighbour who could be used to persuade a statutory tenant to move, releasing accommodation for conversion and re-letting at greater profit. And Rachman was cheerfully unconcerned about overcrowding in his West Indian-occupied properties. The more tenants, the more rents. Desperate immigrants were only too happy to get any sort of roof over their heads.

Michael De Freitas went to work for Rachman as a rent collector. Perhaps as a bully boy. Certainly as the nominal owner or lessee of certain properties: a link in the chain of legal titles by which Rachman kept his personal responsibilities hidden from local authorities. De Freitas may at this time have threatened recalcitrant tenants with knives and dogs. He certainly improved his standard of living.

And he was well placed for a sudden turnaround when it seemed advantageous. In the wake of the Notting Hill race riots of 1958, welfare authorities decided that the causes of black discontent should be investigated. Housing quickly showed up as a priority. And there, presenting himself as a penitent exploiter – and a key witness to expose abuses – was Michael De Freitas. Michael Abbensetts, in his play *Outlaw*, suggests that a quarrel over a woman triggered De Freitas's decisive break with Rachman. But in any event, De Freitas suddenly had a new set of potential patrons: respectable and legally-minded white liberals who urgently wanted to be given an insight into black experiences and opinions. De Freitas had made some impact within the black community by urging at a public meeting that black victims should fight back when attacked by fascist bullies. He had just enough influence to make his claim to be a local community leader plausible. From now on he made sufficient extravagant pronouncements to ensure that the news media's appetite for sensation, added to the gullibility of friendly liberals, would give him a clear run as the most obvious spokesman for the black community.

The 1960s was the period when black protest moved away from the Christian pacifist methods of Dr Martin Luther King to the racist non-Christian separatism of the Reverend Elijah Muhammad's Nation of Islam and ultimately the implicit threat of violence in Stokely Carmichael's Black Power. Respected intellectuals like James Baldwin were having to explain the deep anger underlying these movements to bewildered whites. Michael saw a useful bandwaggon. He could make the aggressive noises and make up the explanations at the same time.

He managed to meet one of the most impressive and influential men of the period, and found a role model. Michael would only be a clay model, caricaturing the role. For Malcolm X's journey from jive-ass juvenile crime to austere self-discipline in the Nation of Islam, and on to a truly Muslim grasp of the brotherhood of man after he had made the pilgrimage to Mecca was one of the great spiritual odysseys of our time. Michael was incapable of taking the first step to follow such a path to wisdom and self-knowledge. But he could copy the externals of the charismatic personality.

He changed his name to Michael X. He made increasingly threatening anti-white speeches. He started a pressure group with the clumsy name 'Racial Adjustment Action Society'. The name was chosen for the acronym RAAS – a decidedly rude word in the West Indies: a metathesis of arse. Michael offered a fancier explanation to white liberals: it meant menses, he claimed, for black blood had always been valued as little as menstrual fluid in white society.

He acquired a building in Holloway, named it the Black House, and announced that he was opening a new black cultural centre. People as distinguished as the Guyanese novelist Jan Carew and as famous as John Lennon and Yoko Ono were taken in and gave Michael active support or financial backing. Actually, Michael's organizations were miniscule shells. But under their cover he could beg for charitable donations. Much of the money was funnelled into drug-dealing and extortion, which continued to supply a good deal of his income, even while his public reputation grew and he was treated increasingly seriously as a black spokesman.

Let's be quite fair to him. He was jailed under the new Race Relations Act for making an inflammatory speech at Reading. There is no doubt that he actually wanted the racial situation to be as tense as possible: it was his personal blackmail hold on rich white liberals. Yet it certainly seemed a scandal that a black man should be the first person jailed under an act intended to protect the immigrant communities. Still, it is usually claimed, now, that he told his audience to kill all white men who went out with black girls – an admonition which would indeed have been outrageous racism (albeit reversing the genders of more familiar previous situations). But what he actually said was, 'In 1958 I saw white savages kicking black women in the streets and black brothers running away. If you ever see a white laying hands on a black woman, kill him immediately.' Overheated language, and an incitement to retaliatory violence, yes. But I don't really think he should have been jailed for it, and I deplore the distortion his words have undergone since his death.

But if Michael's one jail sentence seems undeserved, his continuing criminality was undoubted. He was robbing his 'charitable' organizations rotten. He was sending youths out to steal from shops and supermarkets. And he finally reached a serious confrontation with the law when, under the guise of helping a young black actor who appeared to have been bilked of his rightful earnings, Michael and his bodyguard extracted a small sum of money from an employment agent by using a certain amount of violence and a frightening amount of menaces. Serious charges were brought against him, and Michael knew the carnival was over.

He used the law's delays to strip RAAS and the Black House of all funds, and skipped to Trinidad with a public statement about 'serious differences in the black movement'. The police and serious black activists were relieved to see him go.

In Trinidad Michael was into a new ball game. He could still keep his name before the public – he was in an island where flamboyant characters had been doing this for years, and the press skilfully gave them the newsworthy publicity they wanted without exposing their hollowness. Michael was just one new radical celebrity among many, here. And there was no gullible rich white audience to throw pennies.

Michael changed his name to Michael Abdul Malik, and made links with other West Indians who were changing their names to those of Third World radicals and revolutionaries. Apart from tarnishing the image of the serious left in the Caribbean, these groups had little effect on real politics. Dr Eric Williams, the astute and powerful Prime Minister of Trinidad and Tobago ignored Michael. He neither needed him nor saw him as important enough to need swatting.

Michael rented a new house and an acre of land in a middle class development at Arima. He had an option to buy it after a year. He announced that it was a people's commune and it would help the poor. His handful of uneducated followers were given Robin Hood directions, to steal from their neighbours' gardens and distribute the produce among the poor.

The end was coming fast. With ganja and self-importance clouding his vision, con-man Michael was starting to believe his own propaganda. He thought he counted for something.

His mental deterioration was hastened by the arrival of another black power con-man who had already blown his own mind. Alan Donaldson was very tenuously related to Malcolm X's wife, and peddled this connection for all it was worth to meet rich and influential liberals. He became Hakim Jamal, and wrote a very poor book of reminiscences and race hate. He conned money from Jean Seberg, and arrived in Trinidad having just failed to set up a fraudulent Anglo-Caribbean publishing company, using the money of a young German millionaire.

With him, Hakim brought Gale Ann Benson, daughter of a former British Conservative MP. Like the unfortunate Desiree Malik, Gale Ann had hitched her wagon to a star that was declining from a red giant to a black dwarf.

Hakim had started to believe more than his basic act: he thought he was God. Gale, being in love with him, was the one disciple who convincingly supported this delusion. The only one. There must have been something desperately self-rejecting in her love, for Hakim, though well-made and good-looking, never concealed his contempt for women in general and white women in particular.

In Arima God came up against Michael. And lost. Michael had no intention of acknowledging a superior deity on his commune. Nor would he tolerate a white woman worshipping another black man. Hakim went into a decline and suffered a nervous breakdown.

Michael was tense from money worries. The cash he had embezzled from RAAS and the Black House was running out. And Mr Mootoo who built the Arima bungalow wanted him to complete his purchase or remove himself. The loss of face was terrifying. Michael sent followers to threaten to kill Mr Mootoo. The commune started to brood with death as the end of 1971 approached.

Michael's followers were all very young men. He told them that Hakim was ill and Gale was the cause. He told them her blood must be taken. He imported a rather stupid killer from America who wore African costume and used a Swahili name. Of his own followers, only the fit and healthy Steve Yeates, who had sensed a spark of embarrassing sexual chemistry with Gale Ann, was in favour of the murder. But the others feared Michael too much to voice their own anxiety.

On 23 December Michael gave his male followers fresh blood to drink from a calf the commune had been given for Christmas. Gale, sensing that something was wrong, begged Hakim to leave

Trinidad. She bought two air tickets for them. But Hakim was completely listless and withdrawn.

On 2 January Steve Yeates took Gale to a nearby farm for milk, while the other men, on Michael's instructions, dug a deep hole in the garden, about a hundred yards from the house. When Yeates and Gale returned they went to see the hole, which Yeates told her was a compost pit. Then young Stanley Abbott pushed her in, and the imported American assassin leaped in beside her and began slashing at her with a machete. Knowing that Yeates fancied her, Gale cried out to him, 'Steve! Steve! What have I done to deserve this?' Yeates studiously ignored her until the American's total incompetence became clear. Then Yeates jumped into the pit, seized the cutlass, and drove it deep into her neck. Her arms and body were covered with slashes. The final stab penetrated her chest and lungs. Yet she was still not dead. The men quickly buried her alive, and she expired inhaling the soil with which they covered her. Michael had not been present, but his young male followers were all implicated. The women and children were told that Gale had left. Soon Hakim and the American departed for Boston.

They were replaced by Michael's cousin Sam Brown and a young unemployed barber called Joseph Skerritt. Both were rather surprised to find that Michael's radical revolutionary schemes included half-baked plans to rob a bank for funds. Skerritt also started asking what had become of the white woman who had formerly been such a visible element in the commune. His questions were an obvious danger.

Michael set Skerritt, Stanley Abbott and Sonny Parmassar to dig a 'soakaway' under a sapodilla tree. When it was four feet deep, Michael pushed Skerritt in and killed him with the machete that had killed Gale. Skerritt's last words illustrate the hopeless childishness of Michael's remaining followers.

'Oh, God! Oh, God!' he cried, as blood streamed from his throat, 'I go tell! I go tell!'

His body was covered over, and lettuces were planted on the grave. A few days later the commune members went for a picnic at the dangerous beach of Sans Souci. Steve Yeates, who had grown increasingly depressed as he feared that Gale's murder must ultimately come to light, was drowned while trying to help one of the children who got into difficulties. With the time for Michael to pay the full price of the house approaching, the Mootoo family surprised but unmoved by threats, and Steve's untimely death, even the women and children sensed that the adventure in Arima was turning sour.

Michael prepared to run once more. He moved his most valued possessions into a neighbour's house, left Sam Brown and Sonny Parmassar to clean up, and departed for a speaking tour in Guyana. When he and his family were safely abroad, the house caught fire. There were signs that the fire had been started deliberately, and it seems probable that Michael gave some one else orders to destroy it, since the Mootoos would not let him stay on as a tenant, and he dreaded the humiliation of being evicted.

The police and firemen noticed the lettuce bed under the sapodilla tree. It was far too deep dug and well watered for the crop it carried. Suspecting that it concealed a cache of arms, they excavated. Skerritt's body came to light. More digging in the garden uncovered Gale.

Michael shaved off his beard when he heard the news over the radio in Guyana, and fled to the interior, desperately trying to stumble his way through the forest to the Brazilian border. The would-be charismatic spokesman and leader of black power was a terrified fugitive, quickly picked up by the Guyanese police. Returned to Trinidad he was tried for murder, convicted, and in 1975, hanged.

# 5

# *Marvin Gaye*

Violent killing isn't always murder. It can be manslaughter if death was the accidental consequence of an act of violence which clearly was not lethally intended. It may be justifiable homicide if reasonable force was being used in self-defence. The death of Marvin Gaye was not murder. The court clearly thought it came close to being justifiable homicide. But it was the sudden and violent end of a very sad story, illustrating, again, the fatal potential of the glamorous life.

Think of the 1960s and remember the Motown sound. From Detroit's Tamla Motown emerged Stevie Wonder; Michael Jackson; Diana Ross. Names that have eclipsed all the decade's Liverpool singers except the Beatles.

Berry Gordy formed Tamla Motown to sell black music to a wider market than the black American world and the small company of jazz connoisseurs. And Berry Gordy's first great male performer was Marvin Gaye.

In the 1960s, Marvin Gaye created love duet albums with Mary Wells, with Kim Weston, and, especially, with Tammi Terrel. In the early 1970s, going solo, he perfected the swaggering, erotic seductive style that Lenny Henry beautifully parodies as Theophilus P. Wildebeeste. With extravagant clothes and exaggerated bumps and grinds, he presented himself on stage as a massive macho sex object to his adoring female fans. On stage he would mop his brow with a silk handkerchief, and then toss it into the audience, looking on with narcissistic satisfaction as women scrambled and fought for his sweat. As lyrics became less and less euphemistic, Marvin sang songs like, 'Let's Get It On', and 'You Sure Love to Ball'. By the end of his career he had composed and sung 'Sexual Healing', and only his mother stopped him from issuing 'Sanctified Lady' as 'Sanctified Pussy'.

His unpublished posthumous work included 'Savage in the Sack' and 'Let Me Spank Your Booty (My Masochistic Beauty)'. This was one of the wild ones!

Or was it?

Part of the edge to Marvin's erotic performance was his own self-doubt, and his fear that all sex was sinful. He filled his life with groupies, yet always feared that he could not satisfy them. He married twice. Both marriages ended disastrously, yet both wives continued to obsess him. His first wife was seventeen years older than himself; his second seventeen years younger.

Self-doubt was built into Marvin by his upbringing. His father, Marvin Gay Sr, believed that sparing the rod spoiled the child, and was never satisfied that his leather belt was taking effect until he saw welts rising on his son's body. Marvin Jr resisted, rebelled, and refused to come to heel, but ingested a deep sense of worthlessness, since he felt that he could never win his father's love.

At the same time, he formed the defensive counter-opinion that his father was himself worthless and unadmirable. Marvin Gay Sr held a succession of jobs for a short time, but ultimately allowed Marvin's mother, Alberta, to go out cleaning to support the family. Marvin Sr was a preacher-man in his spare time, expounding and practising a strict and unusual moral code. Marvin was brought up on Seventh-Day Sabbatarian principles: never allowed to go out and play with his friends on a Saturday. In the Washington ghetto, the Gays were among the poorest families, yet they were respected for the different and unusual standards they observed.

And the church tried to force a rigid and impossible code of sexual ethics. Marvin found pubescence difficult. His sexual needs became obsessive, as he despised himself for relieving them.

To make matters worse, his father was an imperfect sexual role model. Not only did recurrent back troubles and sore feet prevent Mr Gay from supporting his family, but ultimately he quarrelled with the church, and resigned himself to doing nothing but sitting around the home, drinking and reading the papers. Marvin despised his father as a bum, yet all his life felt the irresistible appeal of irresponsible loafing.

And Mr Gay was not a macho man. His features were small and delicate; his gestures graceful and almost feminine. His taste in clothes always included something soft and pretty and unmasculine, be it only flowered socks. Marvin, bigger, more ruggedly built, and decisively handsome in a very masculine way, none the less learned from his father the harmless fetishistic pleasure of wearing something feminine. Only he couldn't see it as harmless. He felt it as failure. If the Theophilus P. Wildebeeste act was an act, the audience Marvin most longed to convince was himself.

Even his name invited self-doubt. As he said, you had only to put the word 'Is' in front of it to raise a question in people's minds. He added the final –e to his surname to dispel this nagging anxiety.

So *was* Marvin gay? Certainly not, but equally certainly he was harrowed by fear that he might be.

A man so riven by contradictions was bound to have an up-and-down career. He loved music, and he had learned to stand out in the church as a singer. His father regarded singing as a bum's way of life, and Marvin was able to indulge contradictory needs by becoming a professional musician. He flouted his father's wishes by taking up the 'bum's' life; yet he also proved himself a more responsible man than his father by earning – first enough money, then a lot, and finally a fortune.

And from the time he first started to make money, Marvin was utterly reliable about one thing. He sent money back to his mother. He adored her, and once he was a star, he took over the support of his family, allowing her to retire. His father's life-style was subsidized by Marvin's money, and he silently resented his son's encroachment on his patriarchal position.

Young Marvin clawed his way up through the competitive world of entertainment. Made it to the top. And found, giddily, that there seemed nowhere to go but down.

It was unlucky for him that, just as he reached his pinnacle, Diana Ross broke away from The Supremes to begin her independent career. And Berry Gordy's attention went with her. Marvin Gaye might be the label's male lead, but Diana was the star. Gordy went to Hollywood with her, to see her through *Lady Sings the Blues*. Marvin followed, but never broke into films.

Worse still, up-and-coming younger male singers now overtook him – soon after he had reached success, Stevie Wonder: by the end of his career, Michael Jackson.

Marvin went through hills and valleys of success and failure. He came increasingly to dislike touring, and made a name for himself as unreliable. As he plunged into depressed periods he humiliated his managers; withheld pay from his musicians; fought with his women.

Sex, drugs and money were the principal disaster areas in Marvin's life. His personal sexual kinks found more gratification with the prostitutes he employed relentlessly than with the swarms of groupies he needed to sustain his image. He used enormous quantities of cocaine, spending more money than he dared calculate on the stuff. He turned up at important public occasions, obviously spaced out. And while he earned vast sums of money, he spent them as fast as he earned them.

He was not the first artist to resent the demands of income tax. The hit-or-miss self-employed entertainer who earns fabulous sums one year, and nothing for half a decade, may pay supertax when he is doing well, and then find himself with nothing to see him through the lean times. If the high earner is, like Marvin, also an instant high spender, then the tax-man becomes a nightmare figure demanding vast sums of money and hours of working time given over to uncreative accountancy, sapping the creative energy the artist needs if he is to go on earning. Marvin faced the problem childishly, pretending it simply didn't exist. He just didn't pay his taxes. Vehement protests that the money was only wasted on the Vietnam War and other such evil government extravagances only papered over the fact that he was accumulating anxiety and trouble for himself.

By the 1980s his life was in chaos. He spent periods hiding out and loafing in Hawaii, in England and in Belgium. The taxmen broke into his private studio and his home, removing goods to contribute to the literal millions he owed. Teddy Pendergrass was taking over his public place as the great sex symbol.

The pressures finally produced paranoia. Like other celebrities, Marvin received occasional death threats from unbalanced individuals. He started to take them seriously. He bought guns, and armed his entourage. He feared going out in public without bodyguards. He talked obsessively about death.

Where should a man hide but at home? Marvin returned to the big house at Gramercy Place, Los Angeles, which he had bought for his parents. It was a tense hideout for a sick man.

The house had been bought eleven years earlier, at the height of Marvin's prosperity. With Mr Gay Sr morosely drinking vodka

Parricide Elizabeth Jeffries under arrest with her lover, John Swan.

Richard Dadd, painting in Broadmoor. Notice his extraordinary way of working, right-handed, from the bottom right corner.

Lizzie Borden – 'Look at her, gentlemen!'

Constance Kent confessed that, when sixteen years old, she cut the throat of her half-brother because she disliked her stepmother. She was found guilty, but doubt remains whether she really was a murderess.

William Desmond Taylor as a
serving officer in the Great War: a
photo inscribed for Mary Miles
Minter.

Mabel Normand at the height
of her career.

Friedrich Ritter, the superman crank, with the appalling Baroness
Wagner-Bosquet.

Michael de Freitas, alias
Michael X, alias Michael
Abdul Malik, self-appointed
Black spokesman, con man and
murderer.

Gale Benson, murdered
on Michael de Freitas's
command in Trinidad.

(*Left*)
Marvin Gaye in the years of his success.

(*Opposite above*)
An anti-Catholic medallion showing: (*above*) the Pope and the Devil in attendance; (*middle*) Sir Edmund Berry Godfrey being strangled by two priests and then his body being carried away by sedan-chair; (*below*) the victim dumped on Barrow Hill with his sword through the chest.

(*Opposite below*)
William Wallace on his release after the Appeal Court overturned his conviction.

(*Right*)
Playmate of the Year Dorothy Stratten with *Playboy* publisher Hugh Hefner.

Madeleine Smith – proud, elegant and wicked.

Alma Rattenbury – beautiful and talented.

and insisting that he still ruled a home to which he made little financial contribution, it had hardly been a happy house. But there had been eighteen months respite during 1981–2, during which Mr Gay had gone back to Washington on his own.

Unfortunately, Mrs Gay suffered a severe kidney illness at the time and went to hospital. The entire family resented the fact that her husband neither visited her nor wrote to her. And they were still resentful when he suddenly decided to come back to California and take over his old position as the storm centre, with his moods and his tempers.

For his part, Mr Gay was resentful when Marvin came to live in Los Angeles, making his bedroom a nerve cell of paranoia in the family home. It was not very nice for any of the Gays to have Marvin's seedy drug dealers slipping in and out of the place every day. Mrs Gay was both disgusted by and sorry for the women Marvin brought in – an English girl and a Japanese girl – who were liable to be beaten up when things got on top of Marvin. And Marvin's armoury of guns were not exactly ideal household toys for a 71-year-old Christian lady. Mrs Gay was horrified when she found a machine-gun in Marvin's room, and demanded that he get rid of it at once. Marvin complied by throwing it through the window, and it was instantly stolen from the yard where it lay.

On 1 April 1984, Mr Gay could not find a letter from his insurance company. He shouted at his wife to know where it was. Then he stormed upstairs and berated her. Marvin came into his mother's room and told his father to stop. His father ignored him. Marvin shoved his father out on to the landing and hit him. And hit him again. And again. He was very much the bigger and stronger man.

Mr Gay went back to his own room, and emerged with a revolver that Marvin had given him four months earlier. Mr Gay walked deliberately over to Marvin and shot him in the chest. As his son fell, he shot him again at point-blank range. Mrs Gay ran screaming down the stairs. Mr Gay walked deliberately down to the porch. Threw his gun on the grass, and sat down to wait for the law.

Marvin was taken to hospital and pronounced dead on arrival. Mr Gay's bruises were photographed, and in September, a sympathetic court accepted his plea of 'No Contest' to a charge of voluntary manslaughter. The judge accepted that a father might fear for his life when a strong drug-habituated son started beating him up in a family quarrel. Mr Gay was put on probation.

Marvin Gaye was forty-four when he died.

# 6

## Dorothy Stratten

Although you're extremely unlikely to die by murder, if it does happen, your most probable assailant is your wife, husband or live-in-lover, using an uncomplicated mode of killing – statistically, that is.

Of course, things change if you are a celebrity. Politicians – even Mrs Thatcher – are threatened by terrorists. Glamorous politicians and entertainers may be murdered by deranged loners who nurse a sense of jealousy and alienation.

But what are we to make of the sensational sex-killing of a *Playboy* 'Playmate of the Year': tied up, raped, sodomized, shot dead, and her body sexually abused all over again, by a flashy street hustler who happened to be her *husband*?

Dorothy Stratten's is a very special case. Born Dorothy Hoogstraten in Vancouver, she was an ordinary Canadian High School girl who took a job behind the counter in Dairy Queen when she was fourteen, and found herself still doing the same job while waiting to become a telephonist when she was eighteen. That was where Paul Snider met her. A small-time drugs dealer and pimp who had been out of town for a year, fearing gangland vengeance for a burn, Snider instantly recognized one important thing about Dorothy. She was beautiful enough to make the centre pages of *Playboy* magazine, and a lot of money for her manager.

Now *Playboy*'s critics have many things to say against it, and I shall shortly say several of them. But everyone who has ever met a Playboy Bunny in the flesh admits that the standards of

pulchritude demanded by the organization are extraordinarily
high. And the girls for the centrefolds are without exception
remarkably beautiful. Dorothy was almost six foot tall, slender,
full-bosomed, with the fragile yet healthy little-girlish blonde
beauty that seems to demand protection and admiration at the
same time, and has such a difficult transition to make into mature
good looks without becoming faded. Pure *Playboy* material.

Snider, an experienced technical lover, had little difficulty in
seducing a girl whose only sexual experience had been with a
clumsy adolescent, and he persuaded her that she had found a true
lover and protector. He had more difficulty in persuading her to
undergo a nude photo-modelling session, but in the summer of
1978 she unwillingly agreed. The photos were submitted to *Playboy*
headquarters, and the eighteen-year-old Dorothy and her street-
smart manager found themselves summoned to Hugh Hefner's
mansion in California.

Hefner and *Playboy*, though they played a part in the sexual
liberation of the 1960s, are both true products of the 1950s. Do you
remember the old black-and-white girly magazines? *Health and
Efficiency*, *Spick* and *Span*? Like the ludicrous nudist films of that
era, they featured healthy nubile women catching beach balls and
wielding tennis rackets. They beamed like toothpaste advertise-
ments. And their genital regions were air-brushed into hairless
undivided pads of smooth and seamless flesh. Hefner burst into
this hypocritical market with a refreshing douche of honesty. An
aid to masturbation need not pretend to be a health and open-air
magazine; a nude pin-up should show that she thought about bed.
Glossily photographed in full colour, his 'Playmates of the Month'
set a new standard of less-than-obscene erotica. And throughout
the 1960s, Hefner and his imitators carefully increased the
glimpses of real pubic hair until they had achieved the forbidden
full frontals.

This advance in honesty, coupled with the freethinking liberal
'philosophy' trumpeted by *Playboy* and supported by various
distinguished literary contributors, made the magazine look as if it
was part of the general move into what Roy Jenkins reasonably
called the 'Civilized (rather than 'Permissive') Society'. But it
wasn't really. For, like the 'look-don't-touch' Bunny Girls in the
clubs, *Playboy*'s pin-ups offered titillation rather than satisfaction;
an encouragement to masturbation that could go no further.

And in the Playboy Mansion, partly as a brilliant commercial stunt to show that the glamorous *Playboy* life could be a reality, Hefner, as several commentators have observed, turned his own life-style into a gigantic masturbation fantasy. His outsize circular bed, heated swimming pool and shared jacuzzi baths became famous. The toys of the technical age filled the mansion. Along with girls, themselves reduced to toys. Hugh Hefner had not actually lost his soul to his own fantasy: the old briar pipe and can of Pepsi which seldom left his hands revealed a little core of individuality that rejected the gold-tipped Russian cigarettes and expensive imported whisky from cut-glass one might have expected in the hands of the perfect *Playboy*-man. But on the loudly trumpeted sexual front, the *Playboy* world revealed its shallowness.

Glamour, John Berger has remarked, is the quality of being enviable. To be envied by the lonely men and bored husbands who bought the magazine, life in the Playboy Mansion had to be seen as an endless cycle of promiscuity. And this was not compatible with satisfying relationships.

Even Hefner had discovered this, to his cost. And the need for the Chief Playboy to seem King of the Pack, with every Playmate at his command, like submissive does yielding to the fiercest stag, led to jealousies and competitiveness that the liberated philosophy was supposed to have eliminated. Furthermore, these discontents festered among the rich and successful *men* in the soft pornotopia.

For the optimistic young women, things were even worse. It was all too quickly apparent that they were only esteemed for their looks, nubility and availability. This was a terrible put-down for eighteen- to twenty-year-olds, anxiously searching for a sense of identity. Too many accepted the superficial valuation, and went on to become high-class prostitutes. Too few found the careers in acting and modelling that all the gloss and glamour and exposure seemed to promise.

Dorothy, like so many newcomers to the scene, felt awkward and out of place: affronted by the constant propositions; turned off by the casual and commercial attitude to sex.

But Paul was in his element. The smell of money was all around – indeed, it was heightened and purveyed like a musky after-shave. The trappings of conspicuous consumption were everywhere. It was everything he had ever wanted. And yet his face didn't fit. He lacked the style, the cool, the aplomb of the older, classier males surrounding Hefner. His only ticket to this fantasy-purveying pimps' heaven was attachment to Dorothy. He secured this by marrying her in June 1979.

Dorothy still felt grateful to him. He had brought her more money and excitement than she could ever have imagined in Vancouver, albeit tainted with unreality and a degrading erotic sale of her appearance. He seemed to care for her. He kept her unbalanced, in true Playboy manner, by being unfaithful and jealous at the same time. She thought she loved him.

Nineteen eighty was her big year. And her last. She starred in the sexploitation movie *Galaxina*, and hoped that a career as an actress was about to take off. She was 'Playmate of the Year', and *Playboy* kept her busy with modelling sessions all over the States and in Mexico. And the serious film-director, Peter Bogdanovich, hating the short-term life of promiscuity which followed the breakdown of a long-term relationship, fell deeply in love with her.

Dorothy was too young and too influenced by the fantasy world around her to realize that an honest and open break with Paul was the only clean way out of her predicament. She tried to deceive him, staying with Bogdanovich behind his back. She promised herself divorce in the future, but thought she was being kind by not leaving Paul directly. Of course, she only succeeded in exacerbating her husband's suspicion and jealousy.

He put a detective on to following her around. He started legal proceedings to try and retain 50 per cent of her earnings for life. He recognized that his future on the *Playboy* fringe was non-existent without her, and saw it slipping out of his reach when Hefner barred him from the mansion unless Dorothy brought him personally. He bought a gun.

At midday on 14 August 1980, Dorothy went round to talk to him. Characteristically, she did not tell her lover, Bogdanovich, where she was going. She still hoped that decency and good nature might somehow keep everybody happy and make everything turn out for the best.

We shall never know how the conversation went wrong. Within an hour, Paul had tied her up and abused her sexually, causing her undoubted torment. Then he killed her, removed her body to the bed, and under who-knows-what demons of desire or regret, abused it again. Then he turned his gun on himself and died.

Two tragic victims of the false gods of superficial glamour and loads of money.

*Part four*

# PAST MYSTERIES: RECENT SOLUTIONS

# 1

## Sir Edmund Berry Godfrey

On Saturday 12 October 1678, between 9.00 and 10.00 in the morning, Sir Edmund Berry Godfrey left his home by the Thames and went out toward Marylebone. Within two hours, word reached his brothers in the City that he had been murdered by the Catholics. At midday this report was being anxiously discussed by Sir Edmund's servants and a gentleman with whom he had arranged to dine that night. Yet even while they talked, Sir Edmund had returned from Marylebone and was seen walking along the Strand.

By the afternoon, however, he certainly had disappeared, and during the next five days the story of his secret murder spread all over London.

Late on the morning of Thursday 17 October, the report began to circulate that his body had been found. A strange man announced in a barber's shop that Sir Edmund had committed suicide on Primrose Hill. A man in grey told a curate in a bookshop in Paternoster Row that Godfrey's corpse had been found in Leicester Fields (today's Leicester Square) run through with his own sword.

There are two remarkable circumstances about these reports. Each was independently accurate in one very precise particular: Sir Edmund's body *was* found very near Primrose Hill, and it *had* been run through with his own sword. But, stranger still, both reports were made *before* the body had been found. Somebody well-informed apparently wanted rumour's thousand tongues wagging as fast as possible.

Sir Edmund's body was actually found on the afternoon of 17 October. His sword had been run through him from behind, though there was no trace of bloodstaining on his clothes. Nor did he seem to have fallen on it suicidally like an ancient Roman, for the hilt had made little impression in the soft mud of the ditch on Barrow Hill where he lay. A deep bruise like a one-inch band around the neck indicated that Sir Edmund had been strangled with a ligature before the sword was run through him. Since his cravat was missing, it could be inferred that this was the murder weapon.

In addition, there was heavy bruising on the chest and abdomen, indicating that the dead man had endured a savage beating-up before being killed.

Who was this obscure Restoration gentleman whose death became the talk of London even before it had happened; whose body was described by gossip even before it had been found?

He was a rich and successful coal merchant who became a magistrate. He distinguished himself in 1665, the year of the Great Plague, when most of the Court and gentry fled the city to protect their lives. Godfrey stayed among the dead and dying, and was prominent among the few leading citizens who kept essential services running. For this valuable service he received his well-deserved knighthood.

Yet a few years later he sacrificed the court favour his courage and devotion to duty had won. Despite strong indications of royal displeasure, he insisted on prosecuting a royal physician for debt, and henceforth, though he remained a magistrate and an active vestryman of St Martin-in-the-Fields, he was no longer a coming man or a name to conjure with.

The year 1678 saw his return to some prominence. He was the magistrate chosen by Titus Oates and Israel Tonge to hear their depositions concerning an alleged Popish Plot. And the Privy Council agreed to leave the investigation in his hands.

Titus Oates! There's a truly infamous man for you! A monster of mendacity. An evil perjurer who tossed away thirty-five innocent men's lives and countless good folk's freedom with a reckless disregard for truth, humanity and the eye of God. Compared with Oates, half the murderers described in this book were innocent lambs. Even his parents found it hard to love this long-chinned, tiny-eyed, snot-dribbling cowardly liar. His fellow-men detested him, and he took a frightful revenge, perpetrating the worst political witch-hunt in England's history, and winning for himself short-lived fame as the 'Defender of the Kingdom'.

Oates was expelled from his school, his college, the Anglican clergy, the naval chaplaincy, and two Continental Catholic seminaries for such offences as debt, drunkenness and dissipation, malicious perjury, blasphemy and sodomy.

By 1678 his fortunes were at a pretty low ebb. The only way to make a living that his mean little mind ever contemplated was priesthood of one kind or another. (He might stand as a perfect example of the Quaker principle that no man should ever be ordained to stand between God and the individual or paid to preach spiritual truths, which the apostles offered free to the world. Or the severer Marxist view that priests are parasites, battening on to people's need for assurances going beyond the material, and contributing nothing to the community's economy or the well-being of mankind. But it would be unfair, I suppose, to measure the calling of George Herbert or the Curé D'Ars by Oates's obscene example). After Oates's succession of public disgraces, even the sacerdotal churches wanted nothing more to do with him.

And then he had the good fortune to encounter Dr Israel Tonge.

This elderly Puritan crackpot was a left-over enthusiast from Cromwell's day. He had been lucky enough to remain vicar of St Mary's, Staining in the City of London after the Restoration. But when his church burned down in the Great Fire of 1666, it was not rebuilt, and no one was concerned to find Dr Tonge a new living. With the self-centred touchiness of the true egotist, Dr Tonge concluded that the Great Fire had been started with the primary and deliberate intention of evicting him, good puritan as he was, from the active ranks of the clergy! And who could have had such a diabolical intention? Who but the diabolical Catholics! For twelve years nobody paid any attention to his querulous ravings.

Then, in 1678, Anti-Catholicism became a great political issue. Charles II's brother, James, Duke of York, laid down his high office as Admiral of England, rather than swear allegiance to the Church of England. Here was the proof the opposition needed that James was a secret Papist. Now Lord Shaftesbury and his Green Ribbon Club – the faction that would ultimately become the great Whig party – could dedicate themselves to promoting an Exclusion Bill whose aim was to by-pass James in the succession to the childless Charles, and pass the crown on to the King's Protestant bastard, the Duke of Monmouth.

Nothing could suit the Green Ribbon Club better than a great public scare rooted in the suggestion that all Catholics were traitors. Oates, who had been sneaking a hand-to-mouth existence, saw his chance. Outside Dr Tonge's chambers he hid a set of papers, with forty-three articles outlining an imaginary Catholic plot to kill the King and leading citizens, preparatory to a great Catholic *coup d'état*. It was an easy task to direct the imbecilic Tonge into finding them. And a certainty that Tonge would instantly swallow the poisonous garbage.

Tonge was delighted with this proof of all his suspicions. He pressed the matter forward in two ways. On the advice of certain unspecified 'Very Honourable Friends' he took the papers to the upright magistrate Sir Edmund Berry Godfrey for him to examine. And with the help of another anti-Catholic crank named Christopher Kirkby, he brought the supposed threat to the King's attention.

Now Charles and Godfrey were both intelligent sophisticated men. Sir Edmund took depositions from Oates and Tonge and placed no faith in them. Charles mentioned the purported plot to the Privy Council, but saw little need to follow up the wild accusations. Unfortunately the Duke of York, correctly surmising that political enemies were seeking to damage him through his religion, insisted that the matter be sifted thoroughly. He hoped to uncover and punish the perpetrators. Sadly, his authoritarian zeal rebounded on him (and not for the last time).

The Privy Council told Godfrey to continue his examination of the allegations. Oates and Tonge willingly came forward with the names of more and more trainees for the Catholic priesthood whom Oates claimed to have met in Spain. Rumours about the great plot being investigated by Godfrey abounded, although the enquiry was not coming up with anything very promising. And then, at the end of September, Godfrey, always a depressive, showed marked signs of acute anxiety.

Oates later remarked coarsely that Godfrey was a very great coward, for he had visited him on 28 September and found him trembling and his room stinking as though he had soiled himself. But Oates did not explain this sudden fear.

On 1 October Godfrey told an old friend that he expected to be knocked on the head. He did not say by whom.

On 4 October he remarked, 'I must not talk much, for I lie under ill circumstances. Some great men blame me for not having done my duty, and I am threatened by others, and very great ones too, for having done too much.'

On 7 October he complained, 'Upon my conscience, I believe I shall be the first martyr.'

The following day he asked a widow of his acquaintance, 'Have you not heard I am to be hanged? All the town is in an uproar about me. I took Oates's and Tonge's examinations a month ago . . . yet I have never discovered the Plot they have sworn to. Oates hath forsworn himself, and it will all come to nothing.'

This baffled the widow, but it seems much what the King and the Privy Council had believed all along, so why was Godfrey frightened?

When Godfrey was first rumoured and then shown to be murdered, however, he was indeed adjudged the first martyr of the alleged Popish Plot. His death seemed to prove that Oates's and Tonge's ravings were well-founded, and soon they had found two more perjurers to support them.

Captain Bedloe was a straightforward confidence trickster who spotted the way the wind was blowing, and came forward with false information in the hope of gaining reward money. Roman Catholic Miles Prance was accused of complicity in the Plot and gave evidence (possibly after torture) supposedly confirming Bedloe's. Actually their stories were hopelessly at variance with one another, and utterly remote from the truth. But they served their purpose.

They told an elaborate tale of Sir Edmund's having been lured into Somerset House and murdered there by an Irish priest named Gerald assisted by three of the Queen's servants: Green, Berry and Hill. They, like their mistress, were all Catholics.

Gerald fled abroad. Green, Berry and Hill were arrested, and the bullying Lord Chief Justice Scroggs roared down witnesses who proved, quite convincingly, that they were nowhere near Somerset House at the times alleged. The finger of God was held to point to their guilt, for at that time Barrow Hill, the little rise where Sir Edmund's body was found, just south-west of Primrose Hill, was called Green-Berry Hill. The three innocent men were hanged, and England was plunged into a fearful witch-hunt, with Oates holding a government pension for four years and denouncing whomsoever he chose.

But who really did kill Sir Edmund Berry Godfrey? Certainly no Catholic. Oates's and Tonge's plot was entirely fictitious, and Sir

Edmund both knew it and seemed determined to say so. Yet he feared some great men who thought he was doing too much of his duty. And his death, in the end, was of immense profit to the Protestant opposition. The great scare it kindled enabled Shaftesbury and his allies to introduce their Exclusion Bill. The Dictionary of National Biography suggests that Oates himself lay behind Godfrey's murder – a deduction supported by the simple principle of *Cui bono?*: Who profits?

The late Stephen Knight, who left a bad reputation among Freemasons for his scare-mongering over the brotherhood, and a dubious reputation among Ripper historians for his espousal of the notorious 'Sir William Gull and the Secret Royal Marriage' hoax, did actually do some useful work on the Godfrey case. He discovered a secret service paper listing Godfrey as a member of the so-called Peyton Gang: Green Ribbon extremist gentlemen who had joined with Anabaptists and Fifth Monarchy Men in 1677 in a plot to overthrow the Monarchy and restore the Commonwealth under Cromwell's son Richard. Sir Robert Peyton's twelve associates wriggled out of trouble on this occasion, though six of them lost their public appointments. Now while Godfrey has always been known as a dedicated Protestant, it was not until Knight found this paper that anyone was aware of him as an associate of revolutionary extremists.

One must be cautious with Knight, who jumps to positive conclusions on little or no evidence. But his suggestion that Oates and Tonge were sent to Godfrey by powerful Green Ribbon Men who expected the former Peytonite magistrate to endorse the notion of a Popish Plot is obviously attractive. And one may agree that they would have been disgusted when he refused. We can accept as a speculation (rather than, as Knight offers it, obvious truth) the possibility that they were sufficiently unscrupulous to assassinate a 'traitor' – especially when the deed effectively furthered their faltering cause.

And one may agree with Knight that he discovered a wonderfully appropriate possible assassin in the brutal and bigoted Protestant peer, Philip Herbert, 7th Earl of Pembroke. Herbert was certainly a murderer several times over. He certainly throttled and stabbed his victims after having beaten them up, bruising their ribs and bellies where he put the boot in. Godfrey's corpse *looked* like one of his victims, except that Herbert did not normally use a ligature for strangulation.

Moreover, Herbert's house was in Leicester Fields, associated with Godfrey's death by the extraordinary premature rumour-mongering which really does suggest a large conspiracy lying behind the magistrate's murder. Herbert was definitely capable of any violence. Only, as Knight sadly admits, there isn't a trace of evidence against him in this case. Just the suggestive coincidences.

They make you think, though. *Somebody* murdered Sir Edmund Berry Godfrey.

# 2

## 'Weeping Billy'

Every now and then somebody asks me whether I agree with Colin Wilson's suggestion that sexual serial murder and mutilation is peculiarly a crime of our time: that it springs from the success of technological civilization in satisfying our basic needs for food and shelter, which allows urgency to creep into our more diffuse needs for sexual release, public esteem and dominance.

Like all Colin's ideas, the suggestion is engaging and arguable. It is to some extent supported, moreover, by anthropologist Elliot Leyton's observation that multiple murder is on the increase in certain peculiarly materialist and class-divided modern urban industrial communities, and that the murderers' own words suggest that publicity is as important a motive as sexual release.

But in the end, no, I don't really agree. Leyton (who is badly misinformed about serial murder before the twentieth century) thinks class has as much to do with these murders as the individual psychology, which doesn't quite ring true. Colin Wilson thinks that the Jack the Ripper murders were the first example of sexual serialism, and is certainly wrong. Even the under-informed press of 1888 was able to unearth previous cases in France and Bavaria, and then noticed current examples in Texarkana, Nicaragua and Jamaica.

In the end I suggest that it is our fascination with such crimes that is new. To a greater or lesser extent, the type of crime has always existed, and has, in general terms, been familiar to the relevant authorities. The public was not similarly aware of them. Nor was it especially interested.

Whatever the Freudian consequences of repression, the Victorians and their predecessors were genuinely less interested in sex than we are. A young female victim evoked their sympathy for her compatability with the stereotype of the innocent, blooming maiden. They did not gain a conscious frisson of excitement from the inverted eroticism of contemplating her sexual mistreatment. Consider the case of Elizabeth Winterflood.

That wasn't her real name. She was born Ann Webb. Brought up in the country. And then, like so many country girls, came to London to look for employment around the year 1805.

Covent Garden was the district that made London a Sin City in those days. The fruit and vegetable market had become the accidental centre of the vice trade. For the carters who brought cabbages and cauliflowers from rural England also offered the cheapest form of transport – or even free lifts – for village girls who wanted to come up to town. And, of course, when they practised this eighteenth-century form of 'getting on their bikes', they encountered the usual threat at their destination. Chicken hawks.

The bawds, procuresses and ponces of Hanoverian London gathered hopefully at Covent Garden to await the arrival of fresh virgins along with the fruit and flowers. They offered them secure new jobs; new clothes; a sudden choice between rape or seduction; and soon the helpless and friendless girls were in their toils. Hogarth's Moll Hackabout embarks on her 'Harlot's Progress' from just such a starting-point. And Gay, in *The Beggar's Opera*, writes a poignant lyric pointing to the dual nature of the market for produce and maidenheads.

> Virgins are like the fair flower in its lustre
> Which with its colour enamels the ground.
> Round it the bees in play hover and cluster
> And gaudy butterflies gather around.
>
> But, when once pluck'd, 'tis no longer alluring.
> To Covent Garden 'tis sent – as yet sweet.
> There it grows old and grows past all enduring:
> Rots, stinks and dies and is trod under feet.

We don't know whether Ann Webb was one of the shamefaced

maidens who had let her virginity be plucked and ran away from home to escape pointing fingers, or whether she was one of the innocents seized and debauched on arriving in London with the hope of improving her status as a lady's maid. We do know that by 1807 she had changed her name, and her occupation was unmistakeable.

She worked in the Borough of Southwark. It was a vast sprawling region in those days, embracing all that we would now think of as inner South London: Lambeth, Walworth and Bermondsey as well as Southwark.

Three important prisons or areas of detention for debt lay in the Borough: the Clink, King's Bench and the Marshalsea. Around them (as so often happened around prisons) criminal slums sprang up. Alsatia, south of Union Street, was one area where villains could escape to squalid sanctuary. The Mint around Mint Street was another.

Elizabeth Winterflood lodged in the road we now call Great Suffolk Street. In 1807 it was called Dirty Lane. With very good reason, by all accounts. There was no Southwark Bridge in those days, and no wide Southwark Bridge Street. Dirty Lane was the main route through Alsatia from Union Street to the Borough High Street. Elizabeth lodged near its junction with today's Webber Street – then called Higglers' Lane. Not because the higglers, or street vendors, plied their trade there. But they left their carts there overnight. It was not the heart of Alsatia, but it was a squalid district on the edge of an infamous slum.

In this dismal world, Elizabeth held a very high reputation. Her good country upbringing made her strikingly honest, clean and even refined, compared with the street-smart young whores around her. Her landlady, Mrs Horner, who had no illusions about the nineteen-year-old girl's occupation, none the less called her 'a real lady' – a remarkable description for an urban streetwalker in a run-down district.

By contrast, Elizabeth's ponce, young Thomas Greenaway, was very unpopular with the ladies of the district. His nickname, 'Weeping Billy', suggests a hypocritical and self-pitying unmanliness. I don't suppose anybody living that close to Alsatia was much bothered that he had taken the carpentering skills in which he had been trained and used them to advantage as a thief. A criminal record was part of a good formal education in those environs. Nobody should have found anything odd about his living

under the alias 'William White'. They didn't, after all, despise
Elizabeth Winterflood for the well-known fact that she had
abandoned her given name. And I doubt whether even good Mrs
Horner had much objection to poncing as such. A nice girl like
Elizabeth, the Alsatians would have felt, deserved a good
protector.

The trouble was, Greenaway was neither a good nor a devoted
protector. He ran a stable. And he had the nasty habit of making
them jealous of each other. One of his girls had committed suicide
over his constant infidelities. And now Elizabeth was starting to
feel that she could take no more of him, and they had quarrelled.

One night early in August, Elizabeth went out to work towards
1.00 a.m. Mrs Horner watched approvingly as she stood in a pretty
white dress at the corner of Higglers' Lane and Dirty Lane waiting
for lascivious customers. Mrs Horner was less approving when she
saw Greenaway come up and speak to her. But he moved off, and
the last time Mrs Horner saw Elizabeth, she was on her own again.

At 2.00 a.m. a passer-by saw Elizabeth at the same corner. But
she was no longer standing demurely on the pavement waiting to
offer 'A Nice Time', or whatever the formula was in those days. She
was lying on her back with her skirt pulled up and her legs spread
lewdly apart. The passer-by thought she was a disgusting drunk,
and went to rearrange her dress. Only to find, to his dismay, that
she was dead.

The nearest physician lived in Blackfriars Road. He was
summoned without hesitation, and confronted with something of a
mystery. In the darkness he could not make out what had killed
Elizabeth. There was no apparent blood and no obvious injury,
and it was some little time before he concluded that she had been
strangled.

Meanwhile the aroused neighbourhood had been scouring the
vicinity. Thomas Greenaway was spotted skulking across the road,
but he declined to stay and help the search.

One of Elizabeth's soiled white satin slippers was missing, and
the searchers finally discovered it tumbled under a higgler's cart.
Close to some pieces of flesh.

They took these back to the physician, and he realized for the
first time that Elizabeth had been obscenely mutilated. Her
external genitals had been chopped off and thrown away.

Now what interests me is that *that* fact, which would have drawn
attention to the case today, was of no particular interest at all in

1807. The discovery of the mutilation was no more and no less interesting than the finding of the slipper. What held the public then was the question of Greenaway's guilt or innocence.

He was the only person known to have a grievance against Elizabeth. He had been lurking suspiciously in the vicinity of the crime. He did not give a very good account of himself, and his background was unsavoury. He was arrested and charged with her murder.

Mrs Horner and the neighbours arrived to give evidence against him – vociferously. So much so, that the judge warned the jury to discount their testimony which was transparently based on prejudice. And Greenaway was acquitted.

So who did kill Elizabeth Winterflood? Well, very probably Thomas Greenaway, exactly as charged. Though it makes him unusual. For mutilating sexual murderers don't usually turn their deviance on habitual sexual partners if they kill them. But, on the other hand, sadistic murderers don't usually abandon their practices unless or until they are caught or checked. They may stop abruptly, however, if they know that suspicion rests on them and they are being watched.

There were no more reports of women being killed and mutilated in Southwark. And Greenaway is the only person we are aware of who knew that the neighbourhood and the constables would now be watching all his movements. I think he did it. Wicked Weeping Billy!

# 3

# The Peasenhall Mystery

I was in East Suffolk a couple of weeks ago, enjoying the beautiful spring weather in the unspoilt countryside. Visiting beautiful old houses and cottages in a little village that has hardly grown at all since that day in 1902 which made its name famous all over England. And in the kitchen of seventeenth-century Providence House I looked at an irremovable dark stain on a part of the brick flooring that was once covered by a narrow staircase running up to the attic bedroom. A stain that is almost certainly Rose Harsent's blood.

On the night of 31 May 1902, a tremendous storm raged over the district. At ten o'clock, Peasenhall villagers came to their street doors and looked out, as mighty crashes of thunder approached from the distance. Between 11.30 and 1.30, the storm was overhead. Flashes of lightning scythed down between the clouds. A deluge drenched the main road. The nervous woke up and trembled.

In Providence House, Mrs William Crisp went downstairs to see that everything was all right. Returning to bed she fell quickly asleep, and then was aroused by a crash and a scream from inside the house. What, she wondered, was the matter with the maid, Rose Harsent? Her husband told her to go back to sleep, assuring her that Rose would make her way to their room if something was frightening her.

Early next morning Rose's father came to the house, making his weekly visit to bring her clean linen. He let himself in through the back door to the little kitchen, and was horrified to see his daughter lying dead.

Her throat had been cut. Her head rested against the stairs leading up to the attic where she slept. Her body was almost naked, all but the neck and shoulders of her nightdress having been burnt. There was a strong smell of paraffin in the room, and next to Rose's body stood the kitchen paraffin lamp, separated into three heavily bloodstained parts. A folded copy of last Friday's *East Anglian Daily Times* lay under her head, largely burnt away. The fire which had consumed Rose's nightgown had also scorched the edge of the cloth hanging from the table beside her body. And a bracket supporting a shelf over the doorway to the stairs at her head had broken. Underneath were some pieces of shattered glass which had come from a medicine bottle. The neck of the bottle, with the cork so firmly pressed in that it could not be extracted, had rolled over to the fireplace. It smelt strongly of paraffin, but the label which remained on it showed that it had been prescribed for Mrs Gardiner's children.

Mrs Gardiner! There was a woman whose husband's name was already linked with Rose's. William Gardiner, foreman at the local seed-drill manufacturers, lived in a cottage in the main street just over a minute's walk from Providence House. One year earlier there had been a scandal involving him and Rose. Bill Wright, one of the young men of the village, had seen Rose go into a tiny Congregationalist Chapel opposite the Drill Works to clean it. (The Crisps were prominent Congregationalists, though Rose herself was a Primitive Methodist.) A few minutes later, Gardiner came along and went down the short lane that led to the chapel. He, too, was a Methodist and not a Congregationalist. Wright ran back to the cottage where he boarded to fetch his room-mate, Alphonso Skinner, and the two listened from the other side of the lane.

Both heard unmistakeable sounds of love-making. Then Wright left. Skinner heard Rose make a reference to the 38th chapter of *Genesis* which suggested that she and her partner had just practised *coitus interruptus*. Then Skinner watched Rose come out of the chapel and run away to Providence House, followed by Gardiner, who tip-toed across the road before walking firmly in the direction of the village.

The lads talked about what they had seen, of course, and the Primitive Methodists accepted Gardiner's demand that the story be investigated. In a three-hour hearing at the Methodist Chapel, Wright and Skinner stuck to their story, but the Methodist worthies accepted Gardiner's explanation that he had merely helped Rose close the Congregationalist Chapel door which was sticking, and Wright and Skinner had made up everything else.

The scandal had died down over the year, but now here was Rose lying dead, and a broken medicine bottle from Gardiner's house lying beside her. What's more, the *post mortem* proved that she was six months pregnant.

There was obviously a *prima facie* case for suspecting Gardiner, who fainted when he was arrested.

At his trial, more evidence against him emerged.

An unsigned letter to Rose had arranged an assignation at Providence House for midnight, asking her to leave a light in her bedroom window at 10.00 p.m. if she could manage it. Gardiner had been seen outside his house in a position where he could see Rose's window at that time, and there had been a light in it. A gamekeeper called James Morris passing through Peasenhall at 5.00 a.m. on 1 June had seen rubber-soled footsteps running from Gardiner's house to Providence House and back. Gardiner owned a pair of rubber-soled shoes. A neighbour had seen an unusually large fire in Gardiner's wash-house the morning after the murder, which might explain why no trace of bloodstained clothing was ever found.

Yet with all this evidence running against him, Gardiner's counsel, Ernest Wild, put up a more than spirited defence. Half the village had been in the street at 10.00 p.m. looking out for the storm. Mrs Gardiner had given Rose the medicine-bottle at Easter with camphorated oil for a cold. Rose had happily received suggestive letters and dirty poems from the boy next door, who was just as likely as Gardiner to be her child's father. The rubber-soled shoes in Gardiner's house had come from his brother-in-law and had never been worn. The fire in the wash-house had been the ordinary Sunday morning kettle-boiler.

Wild's best points gave Gardiner an alibi. During the great storm, as was positively confirmed, Gardiner and his wife had sat with a timid neighbour, Mrs Dickenson, not returning home until 1.30 a.m. So Gardiner, it seemed, could not have kept the midnight tryst. And if he had, his footprints would have been washed away in the deluge.

But when the prosecution met this by suggesting that the

murder took place at 2.00 a.m., Mrs Gardiner and the Gardiners' next-door neighbour who could hear all their movements through a thin party-wall, confirmed that Gardiner had gone to bed and stayed there from the moment he came in from Mrs Dickenson's. So it seemed he couldn't have done it.

The complications confused two juries. In Gardiner's first trial, eleven out of twelve were convinced he had killed Rose Harsent; the twelfth said it had not been proved to his satisfaction. Gardiner was tried again, and this time ten out of twelve jurors asserted his innocence. The authorities decided not to prosecute a third time, and Gardiner was released, though hardly without a stain on his character.

So did Gardiner do it? I was taken round Suffolk by two people with a far greater knowledge of the case than my own. Keith Skinner, the Ripper expert, who is also the grandson of Alphonso Skinner (and you should have *seen* the Suffolk villagers giggle and retreat when they learned they were looking at a descendant of the Old Eavesdropper!), and Stewart Evans, a Bury St Edmunds policeman who has made an exhaustive study of the affair.

Stewart shows how Gardiner could have done it. He suggests that the prosecution's error lay in believing the murderer only made one visit to the house that night. Since everyone agreed that Mrs Gardiner went into Mrs Dickenson's house some little time before her husband, William would have had the chance to nip down to see Rose just *before* midnight. And there, in an unpremeditated quarrel he could have killed her.

But fearing that he might have left something to give him away at the scene of the crime, he would have hurried back with the medicine bottle of paraffin as soon as he and his wife left Mrs Dickenson, making the excuse that he was going to the outside privy. He rapidly threw paraffin on the body, started the blaze, and hurried back to his alibi in bed with his wife.

The times fit, and this is the first reading of the facts that really works. Has Stewart Evans solved the Peasenhall mystery? My only doubt is that the assignation note doesn't look like Gardiner's handwriting. As Keith Skinner always says, 'We still want more evidence . . .'.

# 4

## George Harry Storrs

On Friday 10 September 1909, Mr and Mrs George Harry Storrs were entertaining their widowed neighbour Mrs Georgina Macdonald to dinner at their comfortable home, Gorse Hall, above Stalybridge, Cheshire. At half past nine the ladies were sitting at the table waiting for food to be served, and George Harry was in an armchair beside the fire reading a book. Suddenly he saw a figure lurking outside the window. As he hurried over to see who it was, a gun barrel smashed the glass, and a man's voice shouted, 'Hands up, or I'll shoot!'

Undeterred, Mr Storrs continued to the window and pulled the blind down. Two shots rang out – they were not fired into the room, for the blind was undamaged and no cartridges or powder-marks were found – and Mr Storrs would have rushed out into the garden after the intruder had not his wife held him back. Instead, a maid opened the front door a little and rang a handbell for the coachman, James Worrell. Worrell was despatched to the police station in Stalybridge, but by the time constables arrived, the mysterious defenestrator had vanished, and the Storrses were unable to hazard a guess as to who he might be.

The house was relatively isolated in its own grounds. It had no telephone, and the police placed two constables on watch in the grounds at night for the time being. They also endorsed Mr Storrs's suggestion that he should instal a large alarm bell on the roof, with a rope coming down into the attic.

The police may have regretted encouraging this amenity on

29 October. At midnight that night, the bell pealed out across the town, waking most of Stalybridge, and sending half the police force scurrying up to Gorse Hall to see what new outrage had occurred. They found Mr Storrs standing calmly in his door with his watch in his hand. He checked the time of their arrival with the clock in the hall, offered them mulled ale for their trouble, and went to bed satisfied with the result of his little test.

Three nights later the bell sounded again. This time there were no constables in the grounds and precious few in the town to answer its summons. For 1 November was municipal elections night. None of the Stalybridge wards were being contested, so the bulk of the local police had been sent to places where the polls were closing to make sure that the celebration of victory or drowning of sorrows did not get out of hand.

At 9.15, Mary Evans, the cook at Gorse Hall, saw a man in the kitchen. Mistaking him for the coachman, she said, 'Oh, Worrell! How you frightened me!'

Her mistake was instantly rectified as he pointed a gun at her, and said quietly, 'Say a word and I shoot!'

Mary Evans rushed out of the kitchen and into the hall, almost knocking over Eliza Cooper, the housemaid, who was just coming into the kitchen.

'There's a man in the house!' screamed Miss Evans, and fled to the front room.

Miss Cooper gawped after her, and then, like a slapstick victim, was almost knocked over again by a slim young man wearing a cloth cap and muffler who raced after the cook brandishing a gun in his left hand.

In the front room, Mr and Mrs Storrs and their niece Marion Lindley had leaped to their feet on hearing the scream. The cook repeated her breathless message to them, 'There's a man in the house!' And Mr Storrs went firmly out into the hall followed by his womenfolk.

The young man pointed his gun at him, and said, 'Now, I've got you!'

Undeterred, Mr Storrs advanced on him and seized his wrist. As the two men wrestled together, Mrs Storrs ran past them and took down a silver-handled shillelagh that hung on the wall; a quaint souvenir of her honeymoon in Ireland. Seeing the club about to descend on his head, the young man turned to Mrs Storrs and said, paradoxically, 'I will not shoot.'

Mrs Storrs grabbed the gun, thrust her shillelagh into her husband's hand, and raced upstairs to the attic in obedience to his order to her to ring the alarm bell. Marion Lindley, thinking her aunt had gone to hide in a bedroom, ran out of the front door and down to town where she added her incoherent story to the tolling of the great bell. Mary Evans, unwilling to be left alone in the hall with the two fighting men, also ran away: found Eliza Cooper dithering in the kitchen, and hurried her off to the coachhouse to fetch James Worrell.

Unfortunately he was placidly enjoying his pint in the Grosvenor Hotel in town. Nor did he down it in one on hearing the bell. Mr Storrs had cried 'Wolf!' three nights before, and Worrell blandly assumed that 'They must be testing it again.'

By the time help arrived at Gorse Hall, Mrs Storrs had been tolling the bell in desperation for half an hour and her hands had to be prised from the bell-rope.

The kitchen was a grim sight. Mr Storrs lay on the floor, bleeding from a cut over his nose. There were slight cuts on his hands, too. But there was far more blood over the room than could be explained by these minor injuries, Wet patches on his dark clothes suggested that he had been stabbed many times. And not long after he had been moved to a sofa by the window, he died of shock and loss of blood from fifteen separate wounds.

Two men from the Liberal Club, where Miss Lindley was being revived with brandy, were first on the scene of the crime. They both formed the distinct impression that Storrs could have told them who his assailant was when they originally questioned him, but deliberately chose not to, asking, instead, for his wife. Before dying, however, he told the police that he did *not* know who had attacked him.

There was one excellent clue: the pistol which Mrs Storrs had seized and hidden under an upstairs carpet. It was an unusual American make, with the resounding trade name, 'The American Bullock' stamped on it. It was a five-shooter rather than a six-shooter. One chamber contained a rifle cartridge which had been extraordinarily doctored by having the nose cut off to make it fit. And it was less use than a water-pistol. The trigger spring was broken. The swivel-pin between the hammer and the main spring had been removed. The trigger-guard was missing. And the extractor-rod was badly bent.

Unless the murderer had intended robbery, the motive was

utterly mysterious. Nobody knew of Mr Storrs having any enemies. The family generally dismissed the idea that the murderer might have been a sacked workman from the family building firm, of which Mr Storrs was a director.

But the police managed to round up a suspect before long. George Harry Storrs had a disreputable first cousin. Cornelius Howard's father was a pork butcher, famous for his pies. His mother was George Harry's mother's sister. Cornelius, however, had served several sentences for burglary, and had not spoken to George Harry beyond the most casual greetings in the street since his mother's death.

The police hunted for Cornelius and found him, still burglariously occupied, using one of several aliases. They found blood on his trousers and his knife. He gave a patently false explanation of the bloodstained trousers, saying that a pane of glass intended for replacing a window in his former lodgings had broken and cut him. His landlord denied this. The police took him for identification by the women of Gorse Hall.

With differering degrees of certainty, they all identified him, though they all agreed that he had been wearing a light moustache which altered his appearance when brandishing the gun in the hall.

Cornelius Howard was put on trial.

There were three strong points in his favour. The American Bullock pistol could not be connected with him. The women's identifications were really rather shaky. And he could not have been the window-breaking September intruder, who, it seemed, might well have been the murderer casing the joint. For Cornelius had been in police custody at that time, on remand for break-ins committed in Sheffield.

Standing against him was his lie about the blood on the trousers. But he now offered a convincing explanation for this. He had lied because he cut himself on a break-in with which he had not been charged.

He produced a dubious alibi from the landlord of a dubious pub who claimed, with ever-increasing certainty, to remember Howard playing dominoes with three navvies throughout the time of the murder. Fortunately for Howard, the confident police witness who placed the incident one day earlier turned up in court visibly drunk and admitted that he normally consumed fifteen or sixteen pints a day. Cornelius was acquitted, to the delight of the public, which had started to regard him as the snubbed and disregarded poor relation of the miserly and toffee-nosed Storrses of Gorse Hall.

The case was back at a standstill. Then, in June 1910, a young man with a light moustache wearing a cloth cap and a muffler made a murderous attack on a harmless courting couple in a lovers' lane near Gorse Hall. With such brutal observations as, 'I'll cut your f-ing throats!' 'I'll cut your belly out!' and 'I'm going to cut your bloody head off!' young Mark Wilde terrorized James Bolton and his future wife, Gertrude Booth; slashed through Bolton's muffler and stabbed his hand, before running away in the face of Bolton's courageous resistance.

It took the police a couple of weeks to learn that Wilde had been seen hurrying home with blood on his face that night. He was identified by Bolton and Gertie, and convicted of this meaningless assault.

Mr Justice Channel gave him a surprisingly lenient two month sentence for attempted murder. There was a purpose in the clemency. The short sentence kept him in a local prison in Cheshire so that the police had him to hand in their continuing attempts to link him to the Gorse Hall murder.

And very successful these attempts were. The Gorse Hall women made absolutely positive identifications of Wilde as Mr Storrs's assailant. He gave very poor explanations of bloodstaining on his jacket and waistcoat which had appeared around the time of the murder. A bullet, extraordinarily cut down like the one in the American Bullock pistol was found in his house. And that pistol was positively tied to him by the evidence of four ex-army comrades, three of them distinctly friendly to Wilde. They had seen it in his possession with all its identifying flaws and markings.

Wilde asserted that they were wrong. It was a different pistol, and he had kept it on the mantelpiece until his mother objected so strongly that he finally took it apart and threw the pieces away in several places (where they were never found).

His counsel, the rather flamboyant Edward Theophilus Nelson, a Guyanese, was the only black barrister practising in England at the time. He made much of Wilde's having voluntarily directed the police to the doctored bullet. He made absolute hay with the fact that the Gorse Hall women were making their *second* positive identification of a supposed murderer. And, to much public rejoicing, he got his client off.

Today, Mark Wilde seems to have been a very lucky man. He did, in fact, look very like Cornelius Howard in a moustache. His undoubted assault on James Bolton and Gertrude Booth testifies to violent instability in his personality. And the American Bullock might very easily have hanged him – probably would have done – had not Howard been identified first. And crime historian Jonathan Goodman, who has surveyed this incident more fully than anyone else, does not believe that such a hanging would have been a miscarriage of justice. Local oral tradition strongly avers that Mr Storrs had given Mark Wilde a severe thrashing for trespassing during September.

# 5

## Weldon Atherstone

It wasn't his real name. He was born Thomas Weldon Anderson. But he's not one of those suspicious characters with a string of aliases. He was an actor, using the slightly more glamorous 'Atherstone' as a stage name. And he wasn't a murderer. He was a victim.

At about 10.00 p.m. on 16 July 1910, Sergeant Buckley from Battersea Bridge Police Station called at No. 17 Clifton Gardens, Battersea. A chauffeur driving along Rosenau Road half an hour previously had heard two shots and seen a man jump over a wall at the back of Clifton Gardens and run away. Buckley had been sent to investigate.

No. 17 was divided into three flats. The ground floor was empty, but the owner of the first floor flat, a Miss Elizabeth Earl who taught at the (not yet Royal) Academy of Dramatic Art, let him in and showed him through her flat to the back door and the fire escape exit. She and a young warehouseman called Thomas Anderson, who had been dining with her, had both heard the shots and seen a man scrambling over the wall.

Anderson was in the kitchen and joined Sergeant Buckley in the search of the back yard. While Buckley was examining the wall where the intruder had escaped, Anderson heard heavy breathing under the fire escape close to the scullery door of the ground floor flat. Going to investigate he found a man lying there. Miss Earl fetched a brass oil lamp. Buckley examined the body and quickly urged Miss Earl not to come any closer. The man had been shot.

His face was covered with blood and one eye was hanging out. Anderson did not recognize him and was sent back with Miss Earl to wait in her flat for the divisional surgeon and detectives to arrive. Shortly after the doctor had come, the injured man died.

Police immediately noticed something odd. The dead man was wearing carpet slippers. And something odder still awaited them when they went into the locked and empty ground floor flat. His boots were on the mantelpiece, wrapped in brown paper.

Miss Earl and young Anderson confirmed that no one was living in the ground floor flat which was being redecorated for new tenants. But the decorators had left easy means of access for themselves: a string hanging through the letter-box to the latch inside. In the scullery the police found a pair of broken and trampled spectacles. And a bullet hole through the glass in the door.

There had been several burglaries in the neighbourhood recently. Could the dead man have been a burglar?

A search of his pockets revealed evidence that his purposes might have been felonious. In his hip pocket he carried a seventeen-inch length of heavy electric cable wrapped in brown paper and with a woollen wrist-loop attached to one end. A home-made cosh.

His pockets also yielded a diary containing the business cards of 'Weldon Atherstone, Leading Character Actor, 14 Great Percy Street, West Central'. The name didn't mean very much to the police. This 'leading character actor' was, in fact, a very minor comedian who played insignificant roles in music-hall sketches.

Young Anderson was asked to go to the police station to make a full statement. On the way, Inspector Geake asked him if he knew somebody called Atherton. He replied no, but he did know an Atherstone. The inspector showed him the dead man's card and he burst into tears, saying he had unknowingly watched his father die. Then he asked why he was wearing a moustache – was it a false moustache?

The dead man had worn no moustache. It was bloodstaining across his lip, together with the absence of his spectacles and the mutilation of his eye, which had prevented the young man from recognizing him.

Back in Clifton Gardens, Miss Earl, too, lost her composure and went into hysterics on learning that the dead man outside her flat was Weldon Atherstone.

A complicated little situation, well suited to a murder mystery, now unfolded. Weldon Atherstone had left his wife in 1900 and become Miss Earl's lover. The two sons of his marriage, Thomas and William, had continued to visit him and sometimes stay with him in London, and they had met Miss Earl with whom they were on apparently friendly terms. Up to a few weeks previously Atherstone had normally lived with Miss Earl. But a road accident in which he was knocked down and concussed intensified an unhappy suspicious jealousy which characterized the man, and he had broken off the relationship, accusing her of betraying him with some other man. Miss Earl said she had no idea that he would ever come back to her house at night – let alone creep around the empty flat downstairs in carpet slippers.

The two boys who worked as warehousemen had not been party to the lovers' quarrel, and Miss Earl had simply given Thomas supper that night as a family friend. It was true he had gone into her bedroom in the course of the evening, but that was only to see the new decorations she had carried out.

Well! What do you make of that complicated story? Could it be sheer coincidence that Thomas Anderson was visiting his father's mistress at exactly the time that his father was shot in or just outside the house, and that neither of them went down to investigate the shots they heard?

Can you accept that Thomas found his father dying, examined him under the light of a good lamp, yet failed to recognize him?

Could there really be an innocent explanation of Weldon Atherstone's carrying a cosh and changing into carpet slippers with his boots left inside the downstairs flat entirely unbeknownst to his son and mistress upstairs?

Crime historian Jonathan Goodman thought not, and found that Detective Inspector Geake who first interrogated Thomas Anderson had not believed in his innocence either. Geake thought that both Anderson boys and Miss Earl were involved in a conspiracy to kill her lover. The motive was never finally determined, but it could have been an increasing 'toy boy' attachment between Miss Earl and young Thomas, which was hindered by Atherstone's threatening jealousy; it could have been anger on the boys' part at their father's treatment of their mother, leading them to take advantage of the recent breach between Atherstone and Miss Earl; or it might have been a fear on the part of both boys and Miss Earl that Atherstone, whose engagements were becoming fewer and less remunerative, might decline into a sponging dependant. It might have been any combination of all three motives. By this account, William was the young man seen running away by the chauffeur (who quite definitely stated Thomas was not the man) and Thomas's and Miss Earl's failure to investigate the shooting or identify the body was a ploy to give him more time to get away.

But despite Geake's theories, Inspector Badcock, in charge of the case, was unable to bring any charges. And Bernard Taylor believes he was right not to do so. For William was only sixteen – markedly younger than the man seen escaping. And Thomas and William seemed consistently on excellent terms with their father – more so than with their mother. Nor was there any evidence to suggest that Miss Earl's relationship with the boys was other than the innocent one she had described.

No, Taylor suggests convincingly that the paranoid suspicions Atherstone harboured after his accident (and which are well documented in his increasingly pathological diary entries) explain his hiding in the empty flat with a cosh. He genuinely and quite wrongly believed Miss Earl had another lover and was determined to catch him and beat him up.

So did she? And did the two fight? Taylor thinks not. He points out that all Miss Earl's acquaintances were investigated very thoroughly by the police at the time. And he points to the burglaries in the neighbourhood that summer. His suggestion is that Atherstone hiding in the scullery, encountered the unknown burglar breaking in; assumed him to be the imaginary rival, and attacked him fiercely, compelling the surprised felon to shoot his assailant. Goodman had dismissed this possibility on the ground that the man running away was wearing a smart suit, which he thought unlikely for a burglar.

I'm not so sure. Steinie Morrison, a professional burglar of the same period, was a notoriously sharp dresser. I think Taylor is right, and a combination of accident, paranoia and the free life and love style which theatre people have always happily made their own, led to the longstanding mystery of Clifton Gardens.

# 6

## *The Croydon Poisonings*

On Tuesday 5 March 1929 Mrs Violet Sidney died after a sudden illness. She was a hale old lady but she had been grieved by the recent loss of her unmarried forty-year-old daughter who lived with her. Fortified by her religion – an upright and starchy Anglicanism as proper as her straight-backed carriage – and a tonic called Metatone, Mrs Sidney was becoming herself. But just before lunch she complained that her medicine tasted bitter and gritty.

During lunch she felt sick and was unable to finish her oat pudding. After lunch she *was* sick and suffered a sudden and embarrassing attack of diarrhoea. Her surviving children, Tom, an ebullient outgoing concert entertainer, and widowed Grace, both lived nearby. Both were concerned by this sudden illness and they called in the family doctor, Dr Elwell. He and his partner, Dr Binning, suspected food poisoning. But when Mrs Sidney died suddenly that night they had no alternative but to order an inquest, for they were quite unable to specify the cause positively.

Now Mrs Sidney's was the *third* sudden and mysterious death in the family in the space of eleven months. And hers was the second inquest to be ordered.

Edmund Creighton Duff was the first victim – Grace's husband. He was a retired colonial servant, some twenty years older than his wife. He supplemented his small pension with a clerical job at Spicer's the paper manufacturers. In April 1928 he went for a short fishing holiday to Hampshire. He returned with a feverish cold and went to bed. Dr Elwell visited him after supper and concurred that it might be a touch of recurring malaria: nothing to worry about. Edmund was sick and diarrhoeac throughout the night and worse the following day. The doctors were called and took emergency measures to keep his heart beating, despite which Edmund Creighton Duff died at eleven o'clock that night.

Dr Elwell thought the case was probably one of ptomaine poisoning, but neither he nor his partner was certain, so they referred the matter to the coroner. The celebrated pathologist Dr Robert Brontë, the frequent (and frequently humiliated) opponent of Bernard Spilsbury, was called on to make the *post mortem*. He found no signs of poisoning, but sent on samples of various organs for analysis. The pathology labs detected no toxins other than mercury and quinine in medicinal quantities.

At the inquest Dr Brontë attributed death to chronic degeneration of the heart muscle. He believed that sitting fishing in the sun had precipitated a heart attack which, in turn, had caused the vomiting. And that, in its turn, had strained the heart muscle beyond endurance. A sad little story. But there was no need for the family to go on wondering whether Edmund could have eaten bad fish in Hampshire, or whether something noxious had got into the bottle of beer he drank with his supper on returning home.

The Sidneys were a close family and they rallied round Grace, left without benefit of her husband's pension or earnings. His insurance money enabled her to dispose of the remaining encumbrances on her house and move to another in Birdhurst Rise, the same road as her mother and sister Vera. Tom had his own family commitments, but unmarried Vera promised to pay Grace's son John's school fees, so the widow was not left in sad financial straits.

In February 1929 Vera was taken ill. Now Vera was a hearty sporty woman who enjoyed a good round of golf and a good hand of bridge and drove herself independently about the place in her little Citroën car. She had a private income and had no need to work for her living, though, having trained as a masseuse (not, repeat *not* a euphemism for a prostitute in this case!) she took occasional private patients.

In January 1929 she felt a bit under the weather. Typically she tried to shrug it off. On Monday 11 February she had no doubt she was coming down with a bad cold. Again, she tried to treat it by taking a brisk walk in the fresh air. But after dinner that night she was very sick. The next day she stayed in bed complaining that she still felt rotten and the light hurt her eyes.

But Vera was not the only one to suffer from an indisposition that night. Mrs Noakes, the Sidneys' cook-general felt ill after dinner and was sick around midnight. And in the morning it turned out that Bingo the cat had been sick as well. Only old Mrs Sidney escaped this mysterious tummy-bug.

Mrs Noakes put her queasiness down to some rich iced cake she had eaten on Sunday. But Vera felt it was the soup that had made her sick. Usually she was the only person in the house to take soup at dinner: Mrs Sidney didn't like it, and the servant was supposed to content herself with fish and pudding. But the night being very cold, Mrs Noakes had helped herself to a bowl of soup in the kitchen. Finding it tasted bitter, she gave it up after a few mouthfuls and put the rest down for Bingo. H'm . . .

On Wednesday Vera felt a bit better and got up to try and deal with her car's frozen radiator. Her sister Grace called and was surprised to see that she had made such a speedy recovery. So was brother Tom when Vera dropped in on him. He thought she had the gastric flu which was going round.

That day Vera's Auntie Gwen (old Mrs Sidney's sister-in-law) came round for lunch bringing a pineapple as a contribution. When the soup was served, Vera complained, 'Here's this wretched soup again that made me ill on Monday.' Mrs Sidney shushed her, but, as usual, took none herself. Auntie Gwen drank a little soup and then pushed it away. Vera took a little more but still felt it tasted unhealthy.

Auntie Gwen went home early feeling very unwell. She spent six days in bed with a violently upset tummy. Vera took to her bed the next day, seriously ill, and died on Friday. A specialist who saw her on Thursday had no doubt that she was a victim of the gastro-intestinal influenza, aggravated by dilation of the heart brought on by her vehement exertions turning the handle of her cold car on Wednesday. So Vera was buried without any questions being asked.

The questions came, of course, with old Mrs Sidney's death the following month. Her body proved to contain arsenic. So did Vera's. And so, when persistent questioning forced the exhumation of Edmund Duff's body, did her brother-in-law's. The first *post mortem* had been bungled.

So who poisoned this quiet suburban family? They had no

outside enemies and shared no common servant who might have wanted to kill Violet, Vera *and* Edmund. It had to be a family matter.

In fact, as most people quickly saw, it had to be either brother Tom or sister Grace. How do they line up for 'Means, Motive and Opportunity'? Well, both had the opportunity. All the Sidneys were in and out of each other's houses all the time. Tom was slightly better placed for means. All three households kept arsenic in commercially prepared weedkillers. But Grace's was in a liquid preparation which would not have made Mrs Sidney's Metatone gritty and bitter. Tom's was in powdered form, mixing arsenic with caustic soda, and Richard Whittington-Egan, going beyond the call of duty in his investigation of this case, personally sampled both substances. He found arsenic tasteless, but caustic soda . . . gritty and bitter.

But Tom had no motive. While the Sidney in-laws didn't care much for Edmund Creighton Duff who was a bit coarse for their well-bred standards and seems to have made excessive and violent sexual demands on Grace, this hardly gave his brother-in-law a motive for murder.

Grace, on the other hand, was saddled with a physically demanding and financially incompetent husband. He had already lost £5,000 of hers by imprudent investment, and just before his death was planning to cash in his insurance policies, leaving her very insecure. Moreover, it seems she was involved in a liaison with Dr Elwell at the time. Richard Whittington-Egan believes she hoped she might marry the lady-killing doctor if Edmund were out of the way.

And her sister and mother? Well, it seems Vera had threatened to stop paying John's school fees if the Dr Elwell affair went on. And by killing her and her mother, Grace became quite financially secure with what she inherited from them.

The police handling the case had no doubt that Grace did it and were disappointed that the Director of Public Prosecutions wouldn't let them bring charges. And Richard Whittington-Egan, after meeting Tom and Grace and hearing the views of their friends and neighbours, was sufficiently confident to accuse her directly. She didn't confirm or deny it. She gave him a meaningful look, and shut the door in his face.

# 7

## The Wallace Case

These are the facts of the Wallace case. Shortly after 7.00 p.m. on Monday 19 January 1931, 52-year-old insurance salesman William Herbert Wallace left his home at 29 Wolverton Street in the Anfield district of Liverpool, heading for a chess club at the City Cafe, four miles away. Shortly after he left someone telephoned the club from a kiosk outside his home. The caller asked to speak to Wallace, and on being told that he had not yet arrived, asked for Wallace to be given the message to pay him a visit on business the following night at 7.30. The caller gave his name as R.M. Qualtrough and his address as 25 Menlove Gardens East.

About half an hour later the message was passed on to Wallace who seemed undecided whether to follow up the unknown Mr Qualtrough's business or not.

But at about 6.45 the following night he did set out to keep the appointment. Nobody saw him leave or Mrs Julia Wallace say goodbye, although at some time between 6.30 and 6.45, milkboy Alan Close delivered a can of milk to the house and spoke to Mrs Wallace on the doorstep.

Wallace spent a fruitless two hours in search of Menlove Gardens East on the other side of Liverpool. He asked a tram driver for directions and left the tram at Menlove Avenue to enquire again. He asked several passers-by, including a policeman, and called at a Post Office to consult a directory. He went to 25 Menlove Gardens West. All to no avail. For there was no Menlove Gardens East. The recently developed district boasted

Menlove Gardens North, South and West. But no East. Mr R. M. Qualtrough was a cunning gentleman.

At 8. 45 Wallace came wearily back to 29 Wolverton Street. His next-door neighbours, the Johnstons, were just going out when he approached them and said that he'd been out for two hours and now found both front and back doors locked against him. The Johnstons suggested that he try the back door again, and if it still wouldn't open, Mr Johnston would try it with his key. Wallace remarked that his wife wouldn't have gone out as she had a bad cold, and then, on trying the door, exclaimed softly, 'It opens now!'

Mr Johnston said that he and his wife would wait outside while Wallace went in to see that everything was all right. Wallace entered the almost darkened house. And within about a minute he hurried out, saying, 'Come and see! She has been killed!'

Inside the front parlour Julia Wallace lay diagonally across the hearthrug, her feet almost touching the lighted gas fire. Her head had been savagely battered and lay in a pool of blood. Wallace's raincoat was under her head and shoulders.

A small cabinet containing photographs and specimens beside Wallace's microscope had been broken open. A cashbox on the bookshelf, where Wallace normally kept the takings from his collection of insurance premiums, had been robbed of about £4 and returned to its place. A jar upstairs containing a larger roll of notes had not been touched, though there were signs that somebody had been in the back bedroom. There were two spent matches in the parlour doorway.

And those are the basic facts from which the murder has to be reconstructed.

Now the obvious interpretation would be that somebody wanted Wallace out of the way in order to rob the house on Tuesday night, and accordingly set up the phoney appointment with the phantom Qualtrough. And the police did, in the first instance, open an enquiry on a young man who had a criminal record and who, they gathered, would have known the whereabouts of the week's takings in Wolverton Street, and whom Mrs Wallace would have admitted without question. But the young man had some very embarrassing connections from the police point of view and, more importantly, proved an alibi. So that line was dropped, and suspicion turned to Wallace.

What was the case against him? Well, first that he was the victim's husband. Domestic discord is far and away the commonest motive for murder. Never mind that the Wallaces were described as a devoted couple: the outside world doesn't know the tensions that may exist within a marriage and the bottled-up rage that may seethe beneath a calm exterior.

Secondly, the whole Qualtrough business looked very fishy. Since the call had been made from the kiosk close to Wolverton Street, 'Qualtrough' must have seen Wallace leaving the house and making for the chess club just before he made the call. So why didn't he go in and rob the house then and there?

And Wallace seemed to have gone out of his way to draw attention to himself and his fruitless quest for a new customer. He had spoken to a tram conductor and to people in the street, including a policeman. And over and over again he had repeated the non-existent address. Wasn't he trying to force home upon witnesses the idea that he had been on the other side of the city while his wife was being murdered? Didn't the fact that he was a chess player support the idea of a crafty schemer, accustomed to looking several moves ahead, and so advantageously laying the ground for his alibi a day before the actual crime?

Moreover, as his microscope showed, Wallace was a bit of an intellectual even though he had only enjoyed an elementary education. Self-tutored in science, he gave lectures in chemistry at Liverpool City College. He read demanding books and he had recently started to learn the violin which he played to his wife's piano accompaniment. He was an intelligent enough man to plan a perfect murder.

Now what about that macintosh under Mrs Wallace's head? Could he have put on his raincoat to protect his clothes before killing his wife? Might he even have worn nothing underneath it so that there would not be a trace of blood found on him subsequently?

And what about those doors that were mysteriously locked against Wallace when there was no one around but which opened without difficulty as soon as witnesses appeared to prove that he had arrived home to find his wife murdered? Might not Wallace have loitered near the back entry waiting for the first passer-by, so that he was not in the suspicious situation of running out of the house without any proof that he had only just arrived home? The Johnstons couldn't *know* that Wallace had really tried the door previously.

In a normal murder enquiry this would all be preposterous

Agatha Christie stuff, pooh-poohed by any experienced police officer or crime historian. But the curious Qualtrough plot really does move this case, uniquely, into the Agatha Christie field. It happened, and so it has to be explained.

Adding to these clues Wallace's suspiciously calm and controlled behaviour after police arrived at the scene of the crime, they decided that he was their man. William Herbert Wallace was charged with murdering his wife Julia.

But what case can be made *for* Wallace from a scrutiny of the same evidence? First, the fact that the 'calm and controlled behaviour' might as easily result from shock as from guilty calculation. In fact, Wallace had broken down and sobbed in Mrs Johnston's presence before the police arrived.

Secondly, Wallace's intellectual interests – especially the chemistry – gave him ample opportunity to despatch his wife in a cleaner and more comfortable manner. He had sufficient poisonous chemicals in the house to have arranged a death which looked like natural illness and enough intelligence to know it. The Qualtrough alibi was unnecessarily over-ingenious.

Thirdly, the absence of blood was very significant. The raincoat was not bloodstained in such a way as to prove the murderer wore it; it might equally well have been over Mrs Wallace's shoulders as she was attacked (though why it should be has never been explained). The murderer would certainly have got blood over his face, legs and feet, and probably in his hair. The police stripped the plumbing from the house and still found no trace of a murderer's having cleaned himself up.

Finally there was the question of time. The milkboy Alan Close originally said he saw Mrs Wallace alive at 6.45. Even allowing that the Qualtrough alibi meant Wallace had to be pretty nippy, this made it quite impossible for him to get from Wolverton Street to his change of tram at 7.06. Police who tested the route went so fast that they were nicknamed 'the Anfield Harriers'. Their quickest pair had to be completely disqualified as they sprinted for a moving tram: a feat quite beyond an unathletic 52-year-old man with one kidney!

But the best police evidence showed that Wallace *had* to have left the house by 6.50. Five minutes to kill Julia, fake the robbery and clean himself up? Obviously impossible. The police response was to press Close to fix the time as 6.30 and, privately to suggest that what he actually encountered was Wallace, moustache and all, in his wife's clothes, using a falsetto voice!

Wallace was a desperately unlucky man. He lost his beloved wife under atrocious conditions. The cunning scheme used to get him out of the way cast suspicion on him. He found himself charged with murder, and the magistrate who might well have thrown the case out proved (in Jonathan Goodman's words) 'deaf and dim'. At the assizes he was defended by the logical, precise and unemotional Roland Oliver, but prosecuted by a flamboyant barrister, James Hemmerde, who desperately needed a victory to bolster a tottering career, and fought with an unscrupulous determination very uncommon in the prosecution of capital cases. A prejudiced Liverpool jury found him guilty in such flagrant defiance of the evidence that the Court of Appeal, uniquely, overturned their verdict on the facts and not on a point of law. Acquitted, Wallace still faced hostility and suspicion in Liverpool, and died a few years later, a lonely and sensitive man, still grieving for his murdered wife. Even today, when he has been cleared in the eyes of crime historians, he tends to be described by unwitting heirs of post-feminism as a nasty selfish man who let his wife wear old and home-made clothes while spending the family budget on his microscope and general pleasures. In fact, Wallace was a loving and considerate husband by the standards of a time when virtually all men and women took women's household drudgery for granted, and if a man tried to boil an egg he was liable to produce either warmed-over albumen soup or a rubber bullet.

Why do we now see Wallace as innocent? Jonathan Goodman first discovered the original suspect: one Richard Gordon Parry who, as an insurance clerk, had been fired by two companies for petty theft. He had, however, worked under Wallace for a time and visited his house. Furthermore he often came when Wallace was out to sing to Julia's piano accompaniment, and was one of the few people she would have admitted in her husband's absence. He had reason to come on Tuesday and not Monday, for he knew that Tuesday was the day when the maximum premium takings lay in the house, and they would normally amount to more than a measly £4. He was a member of a drama club that used the City Cafe, so he could have seen Wallace's chess tournament fixture posted there. He had a criminal record for theft and violence.

The police discounted Parry when his girl friend claimed that he had spent the entire murder evening with her. They were relieved

to do so. Superintendent Moore headed the case, and his daughter
was Parry's father's secretary!

Goodman traced Parry and interviewed him. He believed he
had done the deed, but could not name him while he lived.

Subsequently Roger Wilkes ran a local radio symposium and
phone-in for Radio City Liverpool (a programme that was also
broadcast on LBC Radio in 1981). He traced Parry's former girl
friend and discovered that her alibi was inaccurate: she had only
been with Parry for the latter part of the evening, not the period of
the murder. And in the follow-up, Wilkes traced a most significant
witness: a garage hand who had washed Parry's car down with a
high-power hose in the middle of the murder night. Parry had
insisted that the interior be hosed as well as the outside. He
grabbed a bloodstained glove which the garage hand found, and
made self-incriminating remarks.

There are a few loose threads still. But enough has been
established to prove that we are very lucky not to have the hanging
of innocent William Herbert Wallace staining the record of British
justice.

# 8

## Maundy Gregory

Perhaps this isn't a murder at all. Perhaps, since somebody died under suspicious circumstances and nobody was charged, this was a near-perfect murder. (In perfect murders, of course, nobody has ever been suspected.)

Certainly, Inspector Askew said that he *would* have charged Maundy Gregory if the man hadn't retreated to France leaving too little evidence for his extradition to be arranged. Anyway, we have a mystery. And a mystery involving one of the most remarkable English rogues of the twentieth century.

J. Maundy Gregory was a parson's son. 'Parson's sons are always the worst,' we used to say at school, without ever specifying what we meant by 'worst'. And at school in Southampton, Gregory teamed up with another parson's son: tiny Harold 'Jumbo' Davidson, later to become a parson himself, and hilariously notorious as the Rector of Stiffkey. (That ought to be pronounced 'Stewkey', but 'Stiffkey', the way it's written is more fun to say.)

Harold Davidson, 'the prostitutes, padre', was to declare that his own personal inspiration derived from Christ's 'attitude to the woman taken in adultery, and still more his close personal friendship with the notorious harlot of Magdala.' (What scriptural evidence is there, by the way, that Mary Magdalene was anything but a perfectly respectable devout woman whose reputation has been sullied by traditional Christian prurience?)

Anyway, with this spiritual example in mind, the Rector spent most of his time walking in Soho and Piccadilly, accosting very young and nubile waitresses, addressing them as 'Queen of My Heart', and offering to put them on the stage. When his upright Norfolk parishioners objected to their Rector bringing young ladies of indeterminate occupation to sleep in the Rectory at Stiffkey, the Bishop of Norwich took up their complaints, and started solemn and expensive proceedings to have little Jumbo unfrocked. Davidson fought his case energetically and passionately, but, with typically outrageous indiscretion, undermined his position by letting himself be photographed in a Soho flat, gazing with undisguised admiration upon a very young girl who had stripped herself naked for his delectation.

Unfrocked and penniless, he tried to persuade the world of his innocence by starting a fast unto death – in a barrel, in full view of the public, in a shop window. (It has been suggested that the public did not see certain large meals brought in by confederates in the small hours of the morning.) Kicked out of the shop, Davidson took his barrel to a sideshow on Blackpool's Golden Mile. And when this proved insufficiently amusing to raise money he started lecturing on his wrongs and his innocence from a cage, which he shared with an old and tired lion. Ultimately the lion became bored, and sank its teeth firmly into its tiresome room-mate. The Rector of Stiffkey expired to the accompaniment of headlines even more ludicrous than those which had accompanied his trial.

This richly comic character shared a passion for the stage with his old schoolmate Maundy Gregory, and early in their careers the two joined forces to promote a revival of the musical *Dorothy*. Its hit song was 'Queen of My Heart', the title which Davidson thereafter freely bestowed on a truly enormous number of attractive young women. Which was very positive-minded of him, for he and Gregory lost their shirts on the show. Davidson had his living in Stiffkey with a handsome stipend of £800 a year to support him. Gregory had to turn to new ways of raising the wind.

He had learned from Davidson the necessary panache for a career as a confidence trickster. He avoided the irresistable impulse to sheer absurdity which undermined his mentor and fellow promoter. And he emerged in the years after the First World War as an apparently very rich man of power and influence.

He owned the Ambassador Club. A successful operation that astutely doubled as a day-time gentlemen's club for civil servants and politicians, offering a good luncheon with bad wine, and at night became a chic dancing and drinking club patronized by the

Prince of Wales. With a good con man's ear for a phrase suggesting insider-status and total discretion, Gregory always referred to the Prince as 'Number One' when he booked a table.

Gregory also owned the *Whitehall Gazette* – a newspaper that imitated the *London Gazette* wherein service promotions and public honours are officially listed. Gregory's paper looked official but was entirely unofficial. It had practically no subscribers and no sales. A print order of about 1,000 copies was almost entirely distributed as comps to centres of the establishment: embassies, and respectable clubs like the Athenaeum. The *Whitehall Gazette* made a little money by publishing regular flattering features on 'Men of the Moment' – from rich industrialists through aspiring politicians to Indian princelings. These instant celebrities paid Gregory generous sums of money to have their names thus brought to the attention of innocent diplomatists and senior clubmen who assumed that the complimentary copies of the *Whitehall Gazette* they found in respectable newspaper racks must have been purchased for some good reason.

But the club and the newspaper were really a combination cover, front and promotional stunt for Gregory's main covert business. As were the lavish Derby Day dinners he gave for very prominent people and politicians. Significantly it was the more brilliant and individualistic politicians who preferred Gregory's company. Men who were not good and loyal lobby fodder and party-liners. Men who seemed dangerously clever to the average plodders. Men like Winston Churchill and F. E. Smith.

And these were also the men who (together with Arthur Balfour and Lord Curzon) favoured a coalition government of outstanding talent, headed by the brilliant David Lloyd George, rather than the dull partisan governments of mediocrities lined up behind Herbert Asquith, Bonar Law and Ramsay Macdonald. Maundy Gregory probably never met Lloyd George. But he was a very important cog in the Welsh wizard's schemes.

Lloyd George's problem was that he had no great party and its bankroll behind him. To fight elections and keep himself in office, he urgently needed a big campaign fund. Maundy Gregory was the discreet Mr Fixit who saw that really big money rolled in to Lloyd George's Fighting Fund without rich industrialists having to offer public support for a man whose policies and personality they probably detested. Maundy Gregory offered a genuine quid pro quo. Titles.

Ten thousand pounds down – as near as dammit in used notes
and brown envelopes – would make you a knight. Not Mr
Hardface Man-Who-Did-Well-Out-Of-The-War, but Sir Hardface. Up the ante, and you could be a baronet. So your son and
grandson would collect the title as well. Sir Hardface II and III. A
good investment. A bit shame-making if it ever came out that you
had really received the accolade for slipping a whacking great tip
into the back of Lloyd George's hand, and not for the publicly
acclaimed service of supplying cheap jam or tin spoons to the
army. But all perfectly legal. And pretty harmless, so far, except for
the distress it might cause people weak-minded enough to think it
matters twopence whether Joe Bloggs is addressed as Joe, or Mr
Bloggs, or Sir Joseph, or Sir Joseph Bloggs, Bt.

The problems came at the next stage up. For considerably larger
sums of money you could buy a peerage. A barony, or maybe a
viscountcy. (Not even Lloyd George dared to flog earldoms or
dukedoms.) But the move from Daddy Warbucks to Lord
Warbucks of Scrooge conferred some real power. Lastingly. On
what might be a pretty undistinguished family. For membership of
the House of Lords gives a vote in the amending debates on real
legislation. Handed down through the generations.

In the unlikely event that a government desperately wanted to
force through a piece of legislation against the advice of its most
experienced supporters in the House of Lords – a new way of
financing local government, shall we say, that is widely believed to
have been discredited in the 1380s – then, who knows, suddenly
hordes of grandsons of the original Lord Warbucks and his ilk
might appear in the Chamber, whipped in by party leaders to
withdraw their attention from the jam factory and the tin spoon
plant for a day, and cast their votes sheepishly on a matter about
which they know little and care less. The older and politically more
experienced aristocratic families, with traditions of *noblesse oblige*
and a primary interest in the Game Laws, were alarmed by the
possibility of irresponsible *arrivistes* changing the nature of the
House of Lords. Democrats who disliked a hereditary legislative
chamber anyway were appalled. And Lloyd George's enemies
were determined to stop him from amassing an effective fighting
fund.

Maundy Gregory was a completely professional covert
operator. He indicated that he was quite willing to bend the club
and the *Gazette* to the interests of any government or powerful

political party that wanted to employ him – even, heaven bless us all, the wicked Socialists! But it was of no avail. His honourable and discreet occupation was declared illegal. The sale of honours was made an offence. Maundy Gregory was a criminal from 1925 on.

It made even greater discretion important. There could be no more of the tax-evaders, dubious financiers and actual convicted criminals who had been ennobled by Lloyd George. But there were still plenty of the 34,000 commoner war-profiteers left to be milked, and Gregory assiduously went on milking them, and secretly buying honours through the whips' offices and the government party machines, until 1931. Then Stanley Baldwin stepped in.

Baldwin had always been a little embarrassed that his family ironworks came out of the war richer than it went in. He had always stood for the safe mediocrities against the brilliant individualists. He set out to crush Gregory and prevent his recommendations from going through. He succeeded in imposing such delays that disaster struck Gregory when one of his clients died before his honour was awarded, and his executors sued Gregory for the return of £30,000 for which no services had, apparently, been rendered.

Gregory could have won a civil case hands-down in court, proving that he had pulled every string on his late client's behalf, and the title would almost certainly have been awarded had he lived. But that would have led to his own conviction under the Honours (Prevention of Abuses) Act, and the exposure and ruin of the business. He had to reach a settlement, and agreed to pay three £10,000 dollops. Only he didn't possess £30,000 cash. And so, in desperation, he made one rash, self-destroying move, and also, possibly committed murder.

The disastrous error Gregory made was to try and sell a title to Lieutenant-Commander Edward Billyard-Leake, an honest sailor who was perfectly content with the DSO his wartime services had earned him, and disbelieved Gregory's initial hint that the government might wish to raise it to a knighthood. When he found that Gregory was trafficking in honours, he simply turned him in and gave evidence against him. Gregory got two months in gaol and a £50 fine. His great racket was over.

But before going to gaol he made one other attempt to raise the wind. For several years he had been living with widowed Mrs Edith Rosse. She was not, as many people subsequently assumed his wife. Nor was she, as they often told landladies, his sister. Odder still, she was not his lover. For Gregory was devoutly homosexual. They really and truly were 'just good friends'. And co-habitees, of course. Occupying the same house, but with separate bedrooms.

Gregory treated her with elaborate old world charm, calling her 'Milady', or 'Little Lady'. They spent a good deal of time at a wooden bungalow in Thames Ditton enjoying jaunts on the river in an electric canoe and a cabin cruiser. And Gregory advised Milady on her investments.

So when the unremitting trustees had seriously narrowed his options, he turned to Milady with a request for a £10,000 loan. And, to his enormous surprise, she turned him down, claiming that she could not liquidate stock from which she drew her income without making a substantial loss. Gregory was horrified. Indeed, the lack of that money led directly to his downfall, compelling him to make the very imprudent approach to Billyard-Leake.

But all did not go well for Mrs Rosse after this contretemps. She fell ill. Sickness, diarrhoea and vomiting. The usual symptoms of a pesky tummy-bug, or an irritant poison.

Gregory was extremely solicitous, and had her attended by an amiable if not over-competent doctor. A brief rest in a nursing-home prompted a quick recovery. A return to Gregory's loving care and home-nursing brought on a relapse.

On the first day of her illness, a blazing August afternoon, with the doctor diagnosing heatstroke, Mrs Rosse announced her belief that she was dying, and asked Gregory to write something for her. And so, on the back of a restaurant menu card, Gregory wrote a will, leaving all Mrs Rosse's property to himself. A more suspicious-looking testament has never been seen. Yet the doctor and housekeeper who witnessed Mrs Rosse's signature both confirmed Gregory's claim that a perfectly sane Mrs Rosse had asked him to write at her dictation, utterly unprompted. And neither had any reason to lie.

On 14 September 1931 Mrs Rosse died. Gregory spent the day in an extraordinary trek around Thameside villages, looking for one with a churchyard overlooking the river. He insisted that Mrs Rosse had loved the Thames so much that she wished to be buried within sight of it.

Most parishes refused to accept the body. Picturesque church-yards are such desirable resting-places that they would quickly be filled with jam- and tin-spoon manufacturers if the vestries did not reserve them for their own resident parishioners. But the parish of Bisham, softened by Gregory's desperate offer of £100 for charity, agreed to let Mrs Rosse lie at the water's edge. Nor did anyone quibble over Gregory's sentimental insistence that he could not bear to think of a great weight of earth laying on Milady. She was buried a mere eighteen inches deep.

But why had Gregory given himself so much trouble and anxiety, haring all over the Thames valley in a taxi, when the bungalow in Thames Ditton gave Mrs Rosse every right to be buried there? Could it be because Thames Ditton graveyard stood a couple of hundred yards back from the river, so that water could not filter through the bank and into the nearby graves when the stream rose? Could he have wanted Mrs Rosse's body inundated as soon as possible?

Three years earlier Gregory had told a friend that he had obtained some curare – a South American vegetable poison. He was most excited by the fact that it would dissolve in water in the body, which meant that it could never be detected, and it could be used for the perfect murder. In the immediate aftermath of Mrs Rosse's death, however, other matters engaged everybody's attention. Gregory faced his court appearance over Billyard-Leake's charge. He had the rum-looking will to prove – he managed it in three weeks. And he had his short prison sentence to serve.

Having paid this 'debt to society' he moved quickly to France, taking Mrs Rosse's money with him. So that he was not available when the lady's niece decided that her aunt's will in her favour must have been clandestinely destroyed. And that her aunt's death was decidedly suspicious. And that the police must be alerted in a remarkable statement that ran to sixty pages.

Gregory was living quietly in Paris when Mrs Rosse's body was exhumed from its scenic grave and Dr Roche Lynch the Home Office analyst stood by to take specimens of the organs and search them for poison. Gregory would not see how completely inundated her grave had been, so that water poured out of the coffin as it was raised. And Dr Lynch, knowing that more poisons than curare dissolve and disappear under the circumstances, muttered gloomily, 'Not a chance! Not a bleeding chance!'

He was right. The examination proved that Mrs Rosse had not died of heat stroke, or a tummy bug, or even Bright's Disease, as her last medical attendant had variously guessed. In fact, it was impossible to say what she had died of. No trace of poison was found. But in that watery grave, this would have been true if she was stuffed to the gills with arsenic.

Did Maundy Gregory get away with murder? His friends thought not. He had neither the nerve nor the heartlessness in their view. The police differed. Had he been in England, they would have charged him with murder. Maundy Gregory died peacefully in France without ever revisiting his native land. Was he a murderer? The judgement of history hangs in the balance.

# Part five
# WOMEN IN LOVE

# 1

# Madeleine Smith

Emile L'Angelier was an ordinary and pleasant young man. Everybody who knew him liked him. But he was unshakeably a nice young man of his time. A conventional young Victorian churchgoer who, faced with moral crises, would feel deep guilt, rush to involve others with him, and cast around to transfer actual blame away from himself, even as he loudly proclaimed his own unworthiness. It's not very unusual. Not very wicked. And not, to us, very appealing.

Madeleine Smith, by contrast, was a thoroughly bad woman. But she was a bad woman in a timeless mould, with all the fatal attractiveness that bad young women possess. She had the bad woman's best and most admirable characteristic: a frank pleasure in her own sexuality and a willingness to grant it satisfaction with any partner of her choice. And she had the bad woman's unacceptable blemish of using her sexuality to manipulate men for her own ends. She lied shamelessly and without hesitation for any purpose that suited her. Her lies were self-interested, putting her in the best possible light at all times. She had no consideration for anyone who crossed her. Honoured no code of family, church or society. And compensated for this moral rootlessness by the enjoyable game of passionately adopting the standards and principles of any lover of the moment. When the lover was discarded, so were the principles.

And when a lover was dead, he was over and done with. When

he was inconveniently alive . . . well . . . that's what made her notorious.

Emile L'Angelier was a Frenchman from Jersey. He had a smart moustache, wore fancy waistcoats, played the guitar, and took a pride in his small elegant feet. He was twenty-eight in 1855. A respectable and charming bachelor whose smart appearance belied his humble occupation as a ten-shilling a week seedsman's counter-jumper.

Madeleine Smith was eighteen. A little plump by twentieth-century standards, but that suited Victorian taste. Emile himself gained dignity in the ladies' eyes from a demure little *embonpoint*.

Madeleine was certainly good-looking. And she was well-bred and well turned-out. She had been educated at a private school in Clapton, and now lived as an eligible young lady at her father's house in India Street, Glasgow. Emile noticed her walking on Sauchiehall Street, and he sent her a single red rose on Valentine's Day.

A few weeks later he managed to get himself introduced to her. And matters moved swiftly.

Emile had a true Victorian's sense of class and boasted of his aristocratic French descent. Madeleine was impressed. Emile told Madeleine he did not approve of her going to dances and parties and flirting with young men. Madeleine, quick to fill her moral vacuum with ideas propounded by personable young men, meekly accepted the lectures. Emile gave her another red rose.

Soon they had kissed. (A big hurdle for two young Victorians.) Soon Madeleine was confessing that she had three intertwined ambitions: to elope; and marry a Frenchman; with a moustache. Emile was in seventh heaven.

Now Mr Smith entered and introduced the missing ingredient to intensify sentimental love. He opposed the match. Emile was not rich enough; his prospects not grand enough. Mr Smith was a successful architect. He had no intention of seeing his daughter entangled with a humble clerk.

Madeleine and Emile corresponded secretly. It added great piquancy to their lives. Emile, indeed, fell desperately in love. And being the basically nice young man that he was, he did not like his passion being a matter of deception. Madeleine assured him that there was nothing to worry about. Her mother knew all about it, and approved. It would all come right for them in the end.

This was a complete lie. Madeleine's first piece of blatant manipulation.

The couple exchanged letters almost daily via go-betweens, and using other people's addresses. Nearly three hundred letters of Madeleine's were ultimately found at Emile's lodgings.

In December Mr Smith discovered that correspondence was continuing. He thundered the outrage of a Victorian papa. Madeleine wrote to Emile that they must part.

Emile wrote furious (and tiresomely moralistic) reproaches. How could she fail in honour? She had promised herself to him.

Madeleine was impressed, and lightly adopted Emile's notion that she must in honour continue as his promised wife. Her letters, ending, 'A kiss. A fond embrace', continued to fuel his passion.

So did their physical embraces. Madeleine wrote how much she enjoyed being 'fondled' by him. But the fondling was starting to give Emile problems. He didn't want to stop at fondling. But he had fully ingested the impossible church law that he and Madeleine *must* stop there. He asked her to help him.

Emile didn't know it, but this was simply enticement to a woman of Madeleine's temperament. The following April their love was consummated at the Smiths' summer home in Rhu.

Now all Emile's unattractive Victorianism contrasts most strongly with Madeleine's appealing universality. She wrote to him:

Beloved, if we did wrong last night it was in the excitement of our love. Yes, beloved, I did truly love you with my soul. I was happy. It was a pleasure to be with you. Oh, if we could have remained, never more to have parted . . . Darling, I love you. Yes, my own Emile, love you with my heart and soul. Am I not your wife? Yes I am. And you may rest assured after what has passed I cannot be the wife of any other but dear, dear Emile. Now it would be a sin.

Emile, of course, thought the sin had already occurred. He wrote:

My dearest and beloved wife Mimi. Since I saw you I have been wretchedly sad. Would to God we had not met that night. I would have been much happier. I am sad at what we did, I regret it very much. Why, Mimi, did you give way after your promises? My pet, it is a pity. Think of the consequences if I were never to marry you. What reproaches I should have,

Mimi. I shall never be happy again. If I ever meet you again, love,
it must be as at first. I will never again repeat what we did until we
are regularly married . . . God forgive us for it. Mimi, we have
loved blindly. It is your parents' fault. If shame is the result, they
are to blame for it.

Well, well, well! What a whingeing mass of self-centred guilt! A sad
Victorian pother. It probably didn't make much sense to Madeleine,
who might have been amoral, but was also a normal healthy human
animal. She entered into Emile's silly game for a bit and refused him
when, inevitably, he made renewed advances. But, naturally, refusal
didn't satisfy him any more than compliance. So she got bored with
him. She simply wasn't a natural Victorian.

But she drifted away from Emile in a thoroughly Victorian
direction. She began to notice Mr Billy Minnoch, a young
businessman with £3,000 a year and the good will of her father. She
set her feet on the slippery slope toward acceptable Victorian
betrothal and marriage, with the full approval of her family.

L'Angelier heard of this, and reacted with great anxiety and
pompous reproaches. She blandly lied to him. But she kept him on
the hook for her own amusement. She wrote to him from bed, in her
nightgown, saying how much she wished he were with her to *love*
[triple underlined] her. And how pleasant it was. And how nobody
who had *loved* [triple underlined] could wish to forego it.

Meanwhile, to speed her betrothal, the Smith family took a new
Glasgow winter home on the ground and basement floors directly
underneath Mr Minnoch's flat.

Emile went on issuing reproaches. So Madeleine tried to break
with him completely. She wrote that he had killed her love. She
asked for the return of her letters and insisted that as a gentleman
he could not in all honour divulge a hint of what had passed
between them.

Emile did not agree with her definition of gentlemanliness. In
his infatuation he believed that they *were* husband and wife in the
sight of God. He believed that her father would now understand
this and approve of their marriage. He proposed to tell him and
show him Madeleine's compromising letters.

This looks at first like nasty blackmail. But Emile was, in fact, fairly
courageous in trying to force a wedding by placing himself in front of
the loaded barrels of the shotgun! And remember, he still believed
that his and Madeleine's love found favour with her mother.

Madeleine panicked. She had to confess that her mother's supposed knowledge of the affair had been a lie, before Emile hurried to enlist Mrs Smith's overt support. She begged Emile not to tell her father. She declared that it was only his reproaches that had temporarily turned her off him. She declared her love anew. She invited him to come and drop letters at her basement bedroom window, and to stand outside it at nights, talking to her. She gave him refreshing, warming drinks of cocoa while he stood outside in the dark.

In January, Mr Minnoch proposed to Madeleine and was accepted. The wedding was set for June.

In February Madeleine bought some arsenic.

She bought it quite openly, in her own name, and signed the poisons book. She told the first chemist she visited that she wanted it to kill rats at Rhu. He asked her whether phosphorus wouldn't be better, but she said they had tried that, and it had failed. The chemist knew her respectable family and that they had a country house at Rhu. He sold her arsenic coloured with soot.

There had, indeed, been rats at Rhu. They had all been killed with phosphorus.

Madeleine went to another chemist and bought arsenic coloured with indigo. For her complexion, she said. She had been told about its use by a French teacher at Clapton. The teacher later denied having told her any such thing.

During February, Emile started to be taken sick after his visits to Madeleine. He remarked that cocoa or coffee seemed to be poisoning him. (But he'd always tended to fuss about his health. Another Victorianism.)

In March he went to Brig of Allan to recuperate. Madeleine asked him to return to Glasgow and visit her. He did not reply. She wrote again, in terms that were bound to fetch him:

Come to me sweet one. . . . Do come dear love of my own dear love of a sweetheart. Come beloved and clasp me to your heart. Come and we shall be happy. A kiss fond love. Adieu with tender embraces ever believe me to be your own ever.

dear fond<br>Mimi

Emile came. He even travelled through Scotland on a Sunday. (Well, he was Episcopalian, not Presbyterian.) He went out for the evening toward Blythwood Square, where Madeleine lived. He returned late at night, very sick. And died the next day, with enough arsenic in him to kill forty men.

At Madeleine's trial, her counsel argued effectively that there was no direct evidence that Emile had seen Madeleine for three weeks before his death. He suggested that Emile had threatened suicide once before when a love affair went wrong. He claimed that Madeleine's passionate summons had actually been a call inviting Emile to learn from her own lips that she was definitely marrying Minnoch! He noted that she had been quite unsurreptitious about buying arsenic.

The judge warned the jury that they must be very careful when the evidence left them to draw inferences. They found the case Not Proven, to Madeleine's outspoken disgust. She had wanted to be cleared completely with a Not Guilty verdict.

Although, as she told H. B. Irving in 1907, she *was* guilty. And she would do it again if the need arose.

But by that time she couldn't even remember poor Emile's name, and thought he was called Louis!

# 2

## Mrs Pearcey

There's a lovely sinister railway arch at Prowse Place in Camden Town. The roadway links Bonny Street and Ivor Street. As you walk under the arch, your footsteps echo eerily around you. If you make an outside broadcast there, as I did once, your voice takes on spooky reverberations.

All very fitting.

In October 1890, Mrs Margaret Eleanor Pearcey who lived at No. 2 Ivor Street (then called Priory Street) was seen pushing a pram under the arch as night fell. The pram seemed very heavily laden. It was covered with a piece of American oilcloth, and the wheels squeaked.

Almost a mile away, across Chalk Farm and near Swiss Cottage, Crossfield Road was being built. There, the next morning, workmen found a body dumped in the middle of the new development. It was a woman in her early thirties. Her head had been battered and her throat was cut.

A mile to the north east of Crossfield Road was a piece of waste land off the Finchley Road, called Cock and Hoop Field. Lying in that field was the body of a six-month-old baby girl, bearing no marks of violence.

Another mile-and-a-half due south lies Hamilton Terrace, Maida Vale. On the pavement outside No. 34 lay a bloodstained perambulator, collapsed after its exertions overnight.

From there back to the sinister railway arch at Prowse Place is two miles as the crow flies, like all these distances. Mrs Pearcey and her pram had taken a very long walk around the south Hampstead district, leaving rather nasty traces of their presence.

The next day, word spread round the north London neighbourhood that a body had been found and needed to be identified. The family of Mr Thomas Hogg, a furniture dealer who lived in Prince of Wales Road, between Kentish Town and Haverstock Hill, were immediately interested. Mrs Phoebe Hogg had not been around to give her husband his evening meal when he arrived home the night before, and a vague suggestion that she might have gone to visit her sister now seemed an inadequate explanation for her protracted absence.

Mrs Pearcey was an old friend of the family. She had nursed Mrs Hogg through an illness the previous Christmas, and she was asked to accompany them to examine this newly discovered body.

Mrs Pearcey was distant and uninterested. When she saw the body she thought it wasn't Mrs Hogg. In the light of her companions' excited uncertainty, Mrs Pearcey's cool detachment aroused police curiosity, and officers went to question her at the *bijou* residence in Priory Street.

There they found evidence of some disturbance. There were bloodstains in the kitchen. A search turned up a bloodstained poker and a bloodstained kitchen knife. The weapons seemed to match the injuries on the body in Crossfield Road.

Mrs Pearcey did nothing to help the investigation, but sat at her cottage piano, humming and strumming. When she was asked to explain the bloody implements in the kitchen, she simply hummed abstractedly, 'Killing mice . . . killing mice . . . killing mice.'

Mrs Pearcey was arrested. And the enquiry now faced the problem of identifying her and establishing the nature of her connection with the Hoggs.

There seemed to be no real Mrs Pearcey. The magistrates heard that she wasn't married at all, but was really a Miss Wheeler. Or that she had married a man called Crichton when she was sixteen, and subsequently adopted the name Pearcey. Would Mr Pearcey or Mr Crichton please step foward, the authorities demanded. The lady refused to help, and these gentlemen in the background seemed very suspicious.

Charles Crichton, a highly embarrassed 'gentleman of independent means' from Gravesend, came sheepishly forward. He paid the rent for the little house in Priory Street. He had supplied the cottage piano. He kept Mrs Pearcey for his personal sexual convenience when he came up to town. And she was, indeed, a Miss Wheeler by law. Pearcey was a Camden bricklayer with whom she went to live for a couple of years when she was sixteen. Mr Crichton knew nothing at all about the Hoggs. What Mrs Pearcey got up to when she wasn't in bed with him didn't concern him. Mr Crichton slunk back into obscurity: the Victorian bourgeois moralist exposed in his true colours.

The connection with the Hoggs redounded to Thomas Hogg's discredit. It appeared that he had been Mrs Pearcey's lover for some time. If Mr Crichton kept Mrs Pearcey for his pleasure, she preferred Mr Hogg for hers. She had given Mr Hogg a key to her house, and he came round for her sexual convenience a couple of times a week.

But she was not his only woman, and it had surprised Margaret Eleanor very much when Mr Hogg suddenly married Phoebe. Still, she ingratiated herself with her rival, nursed her through her sickness, and remained on good terms until, in the spring, it occurred to Phoebe that her husband still had his key to the little house in Priory Street, and still paid it surreptitious visits. There was a considerable cooling of friendship between the two women.

But in October, Mrs Pearcey apparently wanted to bury the hatchet, for she invited Mrs Hogg round to tea. Evidently she doubted whether she would be kindly received if she presented herself at the doorstep in Prince of Wales Road, for she wrote a note and gave a boy sixpence to deliver it while she watched from a little distance to make sure it was received.

Mrs Hogg came to tea bringing baby Phoebe Hanslope Hogg with her in the pram. We don't know what precipitated the murder in the kitchen. We do know that Mrs Pearcey simply dumped her victim on top of the baby in the pram, where her body coincidentally smothered the infant.

Throughout her incarceration, on remand and at her trial, Mrs Pearcey retained her cool air of detachment. The only thing that animated her was the wish to receive support and visits from Mr Hogg. These were not forthcoming. Her actions had, after all, killed his baby and branded him with public infamy. Mr Hogg wanted nothing more to do with her.

Still she hoped that he would come round, and seems to have vaguely believed that he could somehow save her. When he did not, she sent him an astonishing note, forgiving him for deserting her in her hour of need.

Mrs Pearcey was convicted and hanged. A ridiculous suggestion was mooted at the time. Since she had killed a female victim by throat-cutting and dumped the body in the open street, perhaps she had been responsible for the Jack the Ripper murders eighteen months earlier. This was, of course, complete nonsense.

But she left one abiding mystery. Somehow she managed to have an advertisement placed in a Spanish paper telling some unknown person that she had not betrayed him in all her tribulations. Goodness knows what that was all about. At this distance, we can only say that Margaret Eleanor Pearcey was a childishly egocentric woman, incapable of taking anything in the world seriously except her own immature romantic fantasies.

# 3

## Edith Thompson
## and Frederick Bywaters

Edith Graydon was a remarkable young woman. Vivacious and attractive with a shock of thick copper hair, she shone at school, and when she left at fifteen to work for a firm of milliners in the City of London, she rapidly rose to book-keeping and responsibility. By the time she was twenty she was earning more than her father, a simple clerk. She learned French to improve her value to the company. And she read voraciously – crime fiction and romantic fiction, mainly, but also some French romantic fiction with slightly more adult sexual details than the English equivalent.

Her intelligence, personality and ability were remarkable, then. But her tastes, apart from the exercise of linguistic skill, were commonplace.

In 1915 she made the most commonplace and unfortunate decision of her life. She married an entirely suitable young man: a steady worker, a quiet home-lover, a shipping clerk whose plodding character gave every promise of making a good suburban husband. Good, that is, for someone less vital and romantic than Edith.

Percy Thompson's mother objected to the match. She saw, quite rightly, that their characters were incompatible. She objected to the scandalous holidays in the West Country on which Edith took Percy, unchaperoned, while they were still only engaged. But Percy was dazzled and devoted. He was making a terrible mistake.

The Great War did not separate the young couple for long. After a few months in the London Scottish Regiment, Percy was invalided out – not with war wounds, but with a weak heart. Since he smoked fifty cigarettes a day he was certainly not giving that unfortunate organ any assistance, albeit the generally malign effects of smoking were not known at the time. But Percy admitted that his excessive smoking was detrimental to his health.

This was not very good for the marriage. Edith's preferred recreations were active, outgoing and sociable. She enjoyed amateur dramatics, a way of meeting people which is alarmingly conducive to flirtation, and which can usually be relied upon to bring down the disapproval of duller respectable circles.

Percy was of the duller, and would have preferred his wife to stay at home in the evenings. Nor did he approve of her extravagance. While he himself had been a notably smart dresser when they met, by 1920 he would have preferred to see any surplus money in the marriage going prudently into a thrift account. Edith (who, let it be remembered, earned as much as many older men) felt entitled to spend her own money on clothes, and to parade them when she felt like it. After six years, there were no children, and the marriage was settling into that dreary routine of habituated personal unhappiness, held together by a shared economic base, endured by so many couples before reliable contraception, easier divorce, and the public recognition that women can earn and men can cook encouraged more and more people to perceive that convention and virtue are not the same thing.

To the discontented household in Ilford came a catalyst in 1921. Edith's sister Avis went on holiday to the Isle of Wight with the Thompsons, and an old family friend, Frederick Bywaters, was brought along as a companion for her.

Freddy was nineteen – ten years younger than Edith. He was a ship's writer for P & O, travelling on the *Morea* in those years. Since Percy's father had been a master-mariner, and Percy worked for a shipping company, the two men got on well at first. And when the holiday came to an end, Percy invited the young man to come and board with the Thompsons at Ilford.

Freddy was amazed, but accepted with alacrity. For he and Edith had found themselves magically attracted on the Isle of Wight. The holiday had allowed little more than a few stolen kisses. But Edith's romantic temperament and Freddy's youth gave them both the certainty that they had found true love.

The next few months were distinctly fraught. Percy was not blind to the chemistry between his wife and his young friend. Nor were his family and neighbours, some of whom acidly pointed out that Mrs Thompson and young Bywaters were meeting in parks and teashops away from the house.

Finally, on August Bank Holiday, the tension erupted. All three were sitting in the garden when Edith, who probably shared the common feminine view that husbands and lovers are the new substitute for footmen, remarked that she wanted a pin. Freddy leaped up to fetch it for her. Percy sneered at his wife, and when Freddy came out of the house again, a blazing row between the two was under way. When Percy hit Edith, Freddy intervened violently, and Percy responded by throwing him out of the house. There was a month to go before the young man went to sea again, and the lovers embarked on the overheated correspondence that was to bring Mrs Thompson to the gallows.

'Come and see me lunchtime, please, Darlingest. He suspects. Peidi,' wrote Edith on 21 August. 'Darlingest', later abbreviated to 'Darlint', was the way they habitually opened their letters to each other. 'Peidi' was Freddy's pet name for her. Edith's legitimate job at Aldersgate Street gave her an address where she could receive correspondence, and a place where they could meet for lunch breaks and tea after work.

For most of September and October, Freddy was away at sea. On his return, he boldly faced Percy at Ilford, and asked him to give Edith either a separation or a divorce. The older man's first awkward return was perhaps acceptable: 'I don't see that it concerns you.' But his final utterance puts him in a most unfavourable light by today's standards. 'Well, I have got her and I will keep her,' he said: as unlovely a declaration that a spouse is a possession and not a person as has ever been made by a defender of traditional marriage.

Freddy had to content himself with an assurance that there would be no more marital violence, and take himself back off to sea. For a lad of twenty, he was getting into disturbingly deep water, however. Which of us would welcome our young sons rescuing 29-year-old damsels from the distress of marriage to slightly older men?

Mrs Thompson's diet of romantic literature had certainly not prepared her for tactful and responsible correspondence with a young lover. When the *Morea* returned from Bombay and put in at Aden there was a highly disturbing letter awaiting the ship's writer.

He said he began to think both of us would be happier if we had a baby, I said, 'No, a thousand times No' & he began to question me and plead with me, oh darlingest, its all so hard to bear, come home to me – come quickly and help me, it's so much worse this time . . . You know I always sleep to the wall, darlingest, well I still do but he puts his arm round me & oh its horrid.

On arrival at Plymouth there was an even steamier missive.

Darlingest, I've surrendered to him unconditionally now – do you understand me? I think it the best way to disarm suspicion, in fact he has several times asked me if I am happy now and I've said 'Yes, quite' but you know that's not the truth, don't you? . . . If only I had you here to put my head on your shoulders and just sleep and dream and forget. Darlingest come to me soon, I want you so badly, more and more.

As Bywaters' ship sailed and docked and sailed again, there would be a further nine months of this passionate but desperately ill-advised letter-writing. In all, Edith wrote him sixty-two letters: intense, inflammatory, provocative pieces for a young man in love, nearly all of them casting Percy as the coarse brute who stood between them and forced his horrid attentions on Peidi. Bywaters kept them all in his ditty-box.

Edith prudently destroyed all his equally impassioned replies. The one which survives dwells on his intense feelings for her and avoids the subject of Percy's possession. He does, however, seem to have urged her to reopen the topic of divorce, for in one of her letters, Edith refers to a quarrel with her husband in which . . .

I said exactly what you told me to and he replied that he knew that's what I wanted and he wasn't going to give it to me – it would make things far too easy for both of you (meaning you and me) especially for you he said.

But Edith did not restrict her indiscreet letters to jealousy-making accounts of Percy's possessiveness. She also sent her lover a number of newspaper cuttings on poisoning cases. She referred to 'putting something' in the 'stuff' her husband took for his insomnia. She asked Freddy to read up books on digitalin and other poisons. She claimed to have put ground glass and pieces of light bulbs in Percy's food. She asked Freddy to obtain unspecified poisons for her from abroad, and discussed ways of administering them in home-made pills. In short, she stopped presenting Percy as an obstacle to divorce, and started turning him into a suitable candidate for murder.

Had she really tried unsuccessfully to poison her husband? I fear we shall never know for sure. As she and Bywaters are in many ways a rather sympathetic couple, and Percy is portrayed in his wife's correspondence as a boring bear, there is a tendency to give her the benefit of two contradictory doubts. It is suggested that her romantic reading so inflamed her self-image that she *imagined* herself poisoning her husband, though in fact this was merely a piece of play-acting, and she would never actually have harmed him. Conversely it is remarked that none of her alleged poisons would have worked: ground glass and the possible doses of quinine she received from Bywaters wouldn't even have made him uncomfortable.

Now I don't think the lady can have it both ways. If her love of pre-Crime Club fiction led her to play-act the murderess, then equally one might think her reading of Mills and Boon's predecessors led her to fantasize adoration of Freddy. But her love for him seems quite deep and genuine. Although she was sensible and level-headed at her work, she just might have let her emotions override that moral squeamishness which prevents most of us from attempting to kill the most thoroughly unwanted spouses. If she didn't, she was making such a silly pretence that one wonders what was really genuine about her emotional life.

Certainly, if she was completely innocent of attempting to kill her husband, she must be convicted of wantonly and unscrupulously making two men wretchedly unhappy in order to gratify her own sense of drama. But, of course, such conduct is not a crime – let alone the crime of murder.

The end came on 3 October 1923. Edith joined Freddy after work at Fuller's teashop in Aldersgate Street. Then she met her husband and some friends and went to the theatre. At the end of the evening, as the Thompsons were walking home from Ilford underground station, Freddy suddenly sprang out of a side street, started fighting with Percy, struck him twice in the neck with a clasp-knife, and ran off.

'Oh, don't! Oh, don't!' cried Edith, as her secret fantasies, her self-indulgent romanticizing, or her darkest hopes turned into bloody truth. Now she desperately wanted her husband to live. Now she wished her lover had never wanted him dead.

'Why did he do it?' she moaned at the police station. 'I did not want him to do it.'

Freddy explained why he did it. His reasons were as macho as Percy's stubbornness, inflamed by passion though his feelings might have been.

'The reason I fought with Thompson,' he told the police, 'was because he never acted like a man to his wife. He always seemed several degrees lower than a snake. I loved her and I could not go on seeing her lead that life.'

The two were unfortunate in their judge. Mr Justice Shearman fully endorsed the doctrines of marital possession which had turned these two men into a pair of stupid stags with their horns locked in competition for the doe. And possession being nine points of the law he could neither excuse Freddy for taking Thompson's life in trying to take his wife – the judge was perfectly correct in this, of course – nor could he find a good word to say for the wife who wanted to get away. Like a juvenile delinquent New York biker, Mr Justice Shearman might just as well have described women as 'The Property'.

Yet even his savagely prosecuting summing-up did not go as far as the Appeal Court, which actually invented a wholly new and absurd motive for the lovers: a conspiracy to inherit what little money Percy left! With the forces of morality lined up against them, both were hanged.

Bywaters died very bravely, expressing to the end his concern for Edith and his anxiety that she must not be hurt.

Her execution, by contrast, was one of the most obscene occasions of twentieth-century capital punishment. Conscious that she had never prompted Freddy to run out and attack her husband when he did, she knew herself to be innocent of the crime with which she was charged. Vital and young, she could not believe that she was to be extinguished by merciless authority. She was heavily sedated and in a state of collapse, yet still hysterical as she was carried to the gallows. It seems likely that she was pregnant, and aborted as the drop fell. After her execution a discreet regulation laid down that women must wear special leather drawers when they were hanged.

Over twenty years later, when Lady Moseley was imprisoned under Regulation 18B, there was still a wardress in Holloway who was afraid to pass the condemned cell on her own at night, as for her it still rang with the terrible shrieks Edith Thompson emitted after her appeal had been turned down.

# 4

## Alma Rattenbury and George Stoner

Alma Rattenbury was not just pretty. She was beautiful. Her large, deep, misty blue eyes fixed any chosen companion with a warm and attentive gaze. Her full and shapely mouth relaxed easily into a smile at once kind and sensual. Her fine bone structure ensured that her beauty survived the vicissitudes of fashion.

Alma was not only beautiful, she was talented. A gifted musician, she performed as a child prodigy on piano and violin with leading Canadian symphony orchestras in the years before the First World War.

She abandoned her career for marriage in 1913. And a year later, she and her idyllically happy young husband left Canada for Europe and the Great War.

He was killed, of course. Alma, with the courageous resignation of that generation of women, swallowed her personal grief, and devoted herself to nursing at the Front. Before the war ended she met the man who was to become her second husband.

He was rich and well-born: a member of the Pakenham family. Alma was always to marry well, in the worldly sense, though she was never calculating: in no way a vampire or a fortune-hunter. Just a lovely, lively person whose happiness in herself and her companions would always bring joy to those around her. A spoilt child of fortune who, it seemed, would always fall on her feet to the delight of onlookers whom she inevitably rendered generous.

Call no woman happy until she is dead.

Her second marriage didn't really work. She and Pakenham

went to Canada where he was not especially successful as a writer, reviewer and lecturer. She gave music lessons to help their increasingly fraught financial situation. And gradually she became increasingly disturbed by an odd quirk of petty dishonesty in her husband that other friends accepted as amiable eccentricity. He would claim to be an Old Harrovian, though he wasn't; awarded himself an Oxford D.Phil., when he'd never been to the university; and claimed that the fine piano-playing heard from his house was his own, when it was Alma's. At length the marriage broke down completely. Alma moved to Vancouver with her son Christopher.

There she met a much older man, Francis Rattenbury. It was not his wealth that attracted her, though Rattenbury was prosperous: a successful architect who had built the State Parliament and many hotels. But what Alma responded to was the kindest face she had ever seen.

He was fifty-seven. She was about twenty-three. He fell madly in love with her. She had suffered the loss of one adored husband, and the unhappy experience of a short-lived wartime marriage. She was ready to be supported and cushioned by the worship and kindness of an older man.

She gave Rattenbury a new lease of life at a time when he was starting to feel played out and on the verge of old age. He gave her security and modest luxury, together with the passionate support of someone who believed in her and was willing to throw his energies into revitalizing her career.

They returned to England and he took her to music publishers; introduced her to Bert Ambrose the bandleader; successfully launched her as the successful popular song and light music composer 'Lozanne'. They lived in a comfortable but modest house, the Villa Madeira in Bournemouth. Alma had fine clothes, good jewellery, a Daimler and a personal maid, Irene Riggs. It was typical of Alma that Irene became a close personal friend.

But after 1929, things started to go downhill with 'Ratz', as Alma affectionately called him. Though he had a lovely and successful wife and a bright and intelligent little son, Rattenbury's age started to tell on him again. He slipped increasingly into the moods of self-pitying depression which had coloured his life in Canada before he met Alma. He could not bring his old energy to new architectural projects, and after a life of continual success and prosperity, began to worry that his finances were slipping. Alma, who had been brought up in relative poverty, was quite fearless by comparison. But it distressed her husband that her extravagant generosity was unchecked, and she saw no obvious need to stint herself. As he became ever more moody and hypochondriac, they quarrelled occasionally. Once, when he complained that he was going to die, Alma lost patience and snapped back that he'd better get on and do so, then. Which brought him round in a rage, and he hit her. Once only.

For theirs was by no means an unhappy marriage. It had lost its first fine careless rapture, and Rattenbury was becoming an increasingly unhappy man. But Alma still loved him in her easy-going good-hearted way, and cared for him.

Only a new snag entered their relationship. Rattenbury's sexual interest waned under the influence of his age and depression. Alma remained young and vigorous. Ratz was generous. He cared for his younger wife. He urged her to make her own arrangements, and they took separate bedrooms. Alma had always enjoyed a train of admirers, and we simply don't know whether she enjoyed any liaisons prior to 1935. And why should we care? It was their business. Their arrangement. Eminently decent, civilized and unjealous. Only, to quote the terrible, bleak epigraph from Ford Madox Ford that John Irving gives to one of his books, 'All things considered, and in the sight of God, it might have been better if they attacked each other with knives. For these were good people.'

Alma's dreadful mistake was to take into her bed and then fall in love with a boy too young to cope with the decently controlled affections and passions of civilized middle age – George Stoner. The lad with whom her name is forever linked.

It has been suggested that the Rattenburys found it difficult to retain men as servants because Alma tended to make up to them, and that this was why, when they needed a chauffeur-handyman in 1934, they advertised in the *Bournemouth Echo* for a lad, fourteen to eighteen years of age, preferably Boy Scout trained. So George Stoner, a respectable bricklayer's son, came to work at the Villa Madeira.

Irene Riggs was not unduly pleased. Sir David Napley hints that some kind of lesbian attraction might have sprung up between her and Alma, and Irene realized she was about to be displaced. But any good friend might have been disturbed by the Oxford shopping trip.

Alma was in the habit of manipulating sums of money from Ratz on mendacious pretexts (dental and medical care, for example, or visits to relatives) and then using them to go on shopping excursions accompanied by Irene. After Stoner had been working at the Villa Madeira for a month, he was added to the little party going to stay in the Randolph Hotel in Oxford. And on that trip Alma seduced him. She was forty. He was eighteen. She was his employer, a well-to-do, educated, cultivated woman with wide experience of the world. He was a plain, straightforward local lad, with no especial skills. Her situation was transparently undignified and imprudent.

It became worse. Stoner ceased to come in to work daily, but was given a live-in position like Irene's. The Villa had one bedroom downstairs, where Rattenbury slept, and four upstairs. Alma slept in one with little John. Irene in another. Stoner was given a third. He retired to it regularly. But left it just as regularly once the Rattenburys had gone to bed, and joined Alma in her bed.

Predictably this led to some insubordination between mistress and employee; some disputes of a ferocity that should normally have led to his dismissal. Rattenbury, peacefully consuming a bottle of whisky every night in the sitting-room, apparently never noticed. If he did, he apparently didn't care.

In February 1935 a very strange incident occurred. Alma told her family doctor (who was also a family friend) of her liaison. She suggested that though Ratz hadn't been told about it in so many words, he knew all about it and didn't mind. But she also said that Stoner was becoming dangerously jealous, and she thought this was being caused by drugs he was obtaining in London. Dr O'Donnell agreed to see the young man, who told him he was taking cocaine. He said he had found some lying about 'at home' which he had tried. As Sir David Napley has again pointed out, the home in question cannot possibly have been his bricklayer father's; it must have been the Villa Madeira. Moreover, when Stoner was later asked to describe cocaine, he gave a description which conclusively showed he had never set eyes on the stuff. But he may well have had heroin in his hands under the impression that it was cocaine. For he gave a very precise description of that drug when asked what cocaine looked like.

The following month, Alma and George went to London together without Irene. Ratz had been told his wife needed a minor operation for glandular fever.

This time she really splurged. She bought Stoner a complete outfit of new clothes: shirt, tie, grey suit, raincoat, gloves. She bought him hugely expensive silk pyjamas from Harrods. She gave him the money to buy her an emerald ring. To her it was simply giving him what was needed to make good his appearance as her 'brother' when they registered at her hotel. To him, it was obviously a head-turning experience. This lovely older woman had not only initiated him sexually, she continued to take him into her bed and she showered him with gifts. To any cold outside party it looked like a reckless expenditure of Rattenbury's money, obtained on a fraudulent pretext.

And a few days after their return, events took place which ensured that the little jaunt would be exposed to any cold outside parties who could read a newspaper.

At 1.30 a.m. on Monday 25 March, PC Bagwell was sent to a Bournemouth nursing home to investigate information that a man had been brought in with head injuries and foul play was suspected. The man was Rattenbury. The back and side of his head had been battered in, and though he was still alive, his recovery was extremely doubtful.

PC Bagwell went on to the Villa Madeira. There he found Alma in the silk pyjamas and long coatlet which were her habitual housewear. She had a glass of whisky in her hand and appeared drunk. She told him excitedly that she had played cards with her husband until 9.30 and then gone to bed. At about ten o'clock she heard a yell and some moaning, and came downstairs. Ratz was in his chair with blood pouring from his head. She had called the doctor, who took him away.

Bagwell examined the bloodstains on the carpet and noticed that some cleaning up had been attempted. Then Alma made the extraordinary remark, 'I know who done it. I did it with a mallet. Ratz has lived too long. I did it with a mallet.'

She disregarded the policeman's caution, but went on, 'No, my lover did it.' She also remarked, 'I should like to give you £10. No, I won't bribe you.'

If Bagwell had any doubt that she was in fact very drunk indeed, this was allayed when she tried to kiss him. He hurried out into the garden, and Irene Riggs locked all the doors to stop Alma from chasing out after him.

At 3.30 a.m., still very drunk, she confessed again to Inspector Mills, saying, 'I'll tell you where the mallet is in the morning.' When Dr O'Donnell returned from the nursing home he put her to bed with an injection of morphine to quieten her. In spite of which she got herself downstairs again, and told Inspector Mills that she suspected Rattenbury's son. Who happened to be in Canada.

At 6.00 a.m. she awoke, very sick and hung over. She again confessed to Inspector Mills. He thought her condition made the statement worthless, but he noted it down. At 8.00 she repeated the confession, and this time Mills thought it could be accepted as valid. She was taken away, charged with attempted murder, and held in prison.

The police found the mallet which had attacked Rattenbury lying in the garden. Three days later, Stoner told Irene Riggs that he had fetched it from his grandmother's house on the day of the murder. He also made an ambiguous statement to the effect that Alma was in prison and he had put her there. After some reflection, Irene went to the police. Rattenbury died that day, so when Stoner was arrested he was charged with murder.

When he and Alma stood trial together, the case against her looked very black. A drunken and adulterous woman who seduced her servant, defrauded her husband, and then conspired with her lover to put the old man out of the way seemed likely to attract very little sympathy. But a rather different story emerged, strongly supported by Irene and Dr O'Donnell.

Alma, it seemed, really had gone to bed perfectly normally after playing cards with Ratz. It was only after Stoner joined her and calmly informed her that he had killed her husband that she became hysterical. She then made the mistake of swallowing glass after glass of whisky – a disastrous procedure for one who normally only drank a few cocktails about once a month. Her confessions were all to be accounted for by the drink and morphine, which led her to try and protect Stoner.

He, on his side, challenged no part of her story. He did not go into the witness box, but encouraged his counsel to admit that he struck the blows, pleading only that cocaine had driven him out of his mind. Two medical witnesses – one really rather impressive, but the other so hopelessly deaf and decrepit as to do more harm than good – both testified that Stoner struck them as an addict, and the murder was consistent with a drug-inspired frenzy of jealousy.

The jury, the press and the public were all acutely aware that Mrs Thompson had been hanged a few years earlier, as much because she was an adulteress as because she might have encouraged her lover to murder her husband. The judge was not so aware – or, if he was, probably thought it a good thing. Mr Travers

Humphreys made very clear his distaste for women who slept with their servants and spent their husbands' money on silk pyjamas for their lovers. It seemed quite possible that he wouldn't mind seeing Alma hanged for that alone. The jury, thank goodness, kept their heads. They were not overwhelmed by the majesty of the law and the wisdom of the bench. They found Alma Not Guilty and Stoner Guilty. She was free, but reviled.

The judge, the press and even her own counsel suggested that the remainder of her life must be one of shame and repentance. Her home had been exposed as a place where her husband soaked himself to sleep downstairs in the sitting-room while she disported herself with her toy boy in the bedroom where her own child slept. An aroma of drink, drugs and loose living clung to her. And Stoner was to be hanged.

Mrs Rattenbury used her freedom to take herself to a river near Christchurch, Hampshire, and plunge a knife into her breast six times, twice striking her heart.

After that horror, the Home Secretary wisely reprieved Stoner. He served seven years of a life sentence before being released and has led a blameless life ever since.

Oddly enough, two great lawyers of today have come to diametrically opposed conclusions over the case. Michael Havers, the former Attorney-General and Lord Chancellor, concludes that the jury's verdict was absolutely correct: that Stoner committed the murder in a moment of jealous frenzy, believing that Rattenbury might be preparing to prostitute his wife to a rich investor who could help him with his building schemes; and then Alma and George each loyally tried to shield the other for as long as possible.

But Sir David Napley notes professionally that both judge and prosecuting counsel handled their parts of the trial extremely ineptly, while Stoner's counsel was a very poor advocate indeed. (Sir David is a solicitor.) In consequence, Alma's counsel had a clear run. Sir David is extremely suspicious of Irene Riggs and Dr O'Donnell who, he feels, would have supported any story to save Alma. As, gallantly, Stoner did. Sir David, in short, believes that Alma actually killed her husband, and only left Stoner to take the rap when it was pointed out that she had two children to look after. But she could not live with herself when it seemed that this was going to bring her innocent lover to the gallows.

On the evidence given in court, Michael Havers is undoubtedly correct. But Sir David shrewdly observes that the issue of drugs in the Villa Madeira was never properly brought out in evidence, and wonders whether Alma might not have been an addict.

One can only be thankful that the young man was not hanged, as, whoever killed Rattenbury, Stoner had undoubtedly been carried out of his depth by a very lovely and talented woman, quite old enough to know better. And one must regret profoundly the loss of her life, not to mention that of the kind and generous, though tired and depressed Francis Rattenbury.

# 5

*Jean Harris*

On 10 March 1980 Mrs Jean Harris shot Dr Herman Tarnower. She put a bullet through his right hand, another through his chest, and a third (after her pistol had apparently misfired) through his bedroom window. That much she has never disputed. She also shot him in the back, though she declares that she has no recollection of this. One of the bullets that wounded Dr Tarnower has never been found.

Not one of the doctor's wounds was inevitably lethal. But help was slow in arriving, and his removal through a narrow doorway and down a narrow staircase proved difficult, and, through nobody's fault, he died when prompt and effective medical attention might have saved his life.

Mrs Harris's confession to having pulled the trigger took the form, 'I did it! I did it!' It was instantly taken by the police as a confession to murder, and Mrs Harris is now serving a life sentence for murder in the second degree and desperately protesting her innocence.

Dr Tarnower, much as it may pain Mrs Harris to have anyone say it, was an unmitigated heel. He was a wealthy bachelor with a large number of girl friends. From time to time he might propose marriage to one or another. If they were as lucky as Mrs Harris, they might even get an engagement ring. But he always backed out at the last minute.

Nor did he let an old conquest off the hook if he could help it. Mrs Harris became his lover soon after his previous *numera una* —

one of his junior employees – had herself married someone else. But within a surprisingly short time the newlywed lady was back knocking on the doctor's bedroom door, and for the next *ten years* she and Mrs Harris (the *double entendre* is unavoidable) played Box and Cox in the doctor's bed.

Not that they were his sole entertainment. On the exotic foreign holidays he took (frequently in Mrs Harris's company) he would buy jewellery and silk scarves for his other girl friends (often in Mrs Harris's presence). His really close friends were men. Women boosted his ego and satisfied his appetite, though he used plenty of flowers – especially bouquets of red roses – to persuade the more naïve among them that he was capable of love.

His photographs suggest a rather unattractive figure. Tall, angular, bald, with thin lips and a cruel smile. Only once, in a beach photograph in his early days with Mrs Harris, does he look simply happy and contented. Perhaps it is unsurprising that Mrs Harris, though quite willing to bare her soul in her autobiography, never suggests that intense sexual pleasure bound her to this Lothario. Indeed, he seems to have reinforced her rather deep internal contempt for her own role as a sexual object: 'One of Hy's girls', or 'The broad Hy brought along', are ways in which she describes herself in her lover's company.

It was his wit, charm and intelligence that bound Jean to Hy. He was immensely well read and a splendid conversationalist. He had a genuine and sensitive passion for trees; took real pleasure in flowers; and loved oriental art. He collected statuettes of the Buddha. His artistic blind spot was music, which didn't appeal to him. But this was no drawback to Mrs Harris, whose own taste rose no higher than 'golden oldies'.

When Mrs Harris first met him, Hy Tarnower was a rich and successful practitioner. By 1980 he was an enormously rich celebrity. This was because his book, *The Scarsdale Diet*, had become a best-seller. Scarsdale was the name of the group practice Dr Tarnower had established. The diet was basically a one-sheet listing of nutritious foods to enjoy and undesirable foods to eat sparingly which Dr Tarnower followed himself and gave to all his patients. It kept him slim and healthy as he approached the age of seventy, and its sensible intention was, simply, the maintenance of good health (which, of course, rules out obesity.) But the excellence of the diet spread by word of mouth among the doctor's patients and friends, many of whom were foodies whose gross

obsession with *haute cuisine* repelled the less hedonistic Mrs Harris.
The doctor was persuaded to employ an experienced writer to
dress up the diet sheet with anecdotes and jokey recipes and
general health tips. And the book brought the doctor fame and
fortune.

By 1980 Mrs Harris was suffering from severe stress. She had
divorced an entirely amiable but apparently unexciting first
husband in 1960 when she realized that being a housewife bored
her. She became a teacher in the American private school system.
It offered lower salaries but more opportunity for dedicated
teaching than the public schools. Mrs Harris was – is – a gifted and
sympathetic teacher, a serious and dedicated person, and an
achiever. By the 1970s when she had already become Dr
Tarnower's lover, she rose to become a school's headmistress.

She herself admits that something like the Peter Principle may
have come into play here: that she let the salary increase attract her
into promotion beyond her maximum level of competence. Not that
she was a bad headmistress. But her personality makes her at one and
the same time unwilling to compromise on issues of principle, and far
too sensitive to withstand the opposition and criticism this inevitably
evokes. A more rhinoceros-hided woman might have marched on
from strength to strength, with complaining parents and governors
forced to fall into line as she created the type of school she wanted. A
woman who yielded more for a quiet life might have watched her
school's decline, but she would not have wound herself up to such a
point that she drove from Virginia to New York to carry a loaded
pistol into her lover's bedroom.

Hy Tarnower had not used his medical skills to help Mrs
Harris's stress. Apparently he liked his broads peppy rather than
overworked, and he prescribed speed for her for ten years, without
her having any idea what it was.

Yet it seemed to her that Hy was keeping her sane. Weekends at
his comfortable house in New York were a blessed relief from the
pressures of School Board, the complaints of alumni who wanted
everything done just as it had been thirty years earlier, the
indignation of parents who wanted pot-smoking suppressed just as
long as the suppression didn't involve the suspension of *their*
daughters, and the sullenness of girls who thought that a private
school's priorities ought to recognize horse-riding as more
important than academic study.

Holidays abroad with Hy were an even more complete break.

And those holidays might have made many women drag on the increasingly unsatisfactory relationship. Bangkok, Khartoum, Jiddah – you name the exciting locality off, or only just coming on the tourist trail – and there the couple were. With more conventional bouts of off-season sunshine in Florida and the Caribbean. Trips like that more than once a year would make me seriously consider becoming a toy boy for some extravagant old lady – wouldn't you?

But this good life was drawing to a close by 1980. Hy bothered less and less about removing other women's clothes and property from his bedroom when Jean came up for the weekend. He was less and less interested in taking her globe-trotting. She was forced into the humiliating recognition that she was merely a tolerated presence around a man she loved. And that a rival she loathed was enjoying centre-stage.

What's the masculine equivalent of a bitch? Whatever the word is, Hy Tarnower obviously found it very comfortable to have women hating each other over him.

On 20 March Mrs Harris snapped. It was a bad day at school. She felt she could take no more appointments and cancelled the end of her working day. She rang Hy to tell him she wanted to come up to New York to get away from it all. His evasive response proved that he expected her rival there overnight. Mrs Harris dug her heels in. She said she was coming, anyway. But Hy's offhandedness was the last straw.

She made her will and got her secretarial staff to witness it. She loaded her gun with considerable difficulty, leaving one chamber accidentally empty. She wrote three suicide notes. She rang Hy again to confirm that she was coming. And she drove north.

The house was in darkness when she arrived: even the front porch light had not been left on for her. Mrs Harris knew her way in through the garage, however, and taking her handbag with the pistol in it, made her way straight up to Hy's bedroom. He was asleep alone, but woke up when she turned the light on. What happened next can only be described by Mrs Harris. No one else was there.

She says it had always been her intention to have a few peaceful words with Hy and then, without warning him, go out quietly to his garden and shoot herself. But Hy, waking irritably as the light went on, was in no mood for conversation, and simply said, 'Jesus, Jean! Go to bed!'

She could not persuade him to talk. And she lost her cool completely when she went into the bathroom and found her rival's nightdress and toilet things lying around. She tore up the nightdress and threw the toilet things out of the window. Hy got out of bed and slapped her. Maybe he was just an antediluvian doctor thinking he was effectively checking hysteria. But Mrs Harris thought it was real anger and she decided, then and there, to shoot herself in the bedroom.

When Hy saw the pistol come out of her handbag, he raced across the room to take it from her, batting at it to knock it out of her grasp. That was when it first went off and blew a hole right through his hand. With cultivated understatement, he said, 'Jesus, Jean! Look what you've done!' Then he padded over to the bathroom, dripping blood, to wash his wound.

On his return, he realized that she had picked up the gun again, and was pointing it at herself. Using all his strength, he grabbed her upper arm and made her drop it. They struggled and scrambled for it, and both their hands were on it when Mrs Harris felt the muzzle pointing into her own stomach, and forced the trigger.

The explosion rocked her, but she felt no pain, and says she wondered why she'd never killed herself before if it made so little difference to what she felt like. Then she realized that it was not the muzzle, but the butt which had been jabbing into her. Hy was staggering away to his bed, bleeding from the chest.

At this point she aimed the pistol firmly at her own head and pulled the trigger. It merely clicked. The empty chamber had come round.

Thinking it was broken, she pointed it at random in the air and pulled the trigger several times, getting only irritating click-clicks in response. Until it went off and a bullet flew through the window. Presumably it was at this time that one of her bullets entered Hy's back.

She made a last struggle to reload the gun, but damaged it in so doing, and finally realized that Hy was seriously hurt. The servants hadn't answered his buzz for assistance when the first bullet struck his hand, and Hy and Jean assumed the staff intercom was out of order. Eventually Mrs Harris drove out to a phone box to summon the police and an ambulance, and in a state of complete shock made her damning confession, 'I did it! I did it!'

Her suicide notes, which might have cleared her, were

unfortunately ambiguous. The prosecution case at the trial contained a nasty quantity of revised and altered testimony, and some medical evidence so flaky that it evoked an article of protest in a learned journal. Mrs Harris's lawyer was handicapped by her insistence that Hy should not be presented as an out-and-out cad, as this was not the very complex truth as she saw it.

The prosecution was hampered by no such scruples, and went all out for victory with a simple and easily understandable story of 'Hell hath no fury like a woman scorned.' The press made the most of a 'socialite' headmistress of fifty-nine daring to fornicate with a rich celebrity of sixty-nine. And the bullet in Hy's back, which Mrs Harris remembered nothing about, would have been a nasty point for any defending lawyer to deal with.

Nevertheless, I have no doubt at all that Marshall Hall would have got her off. Handguns held by tense women in lovers' quarrels were his speciality. Why, Sir Patrick Hastings even got Mrs Barney off under much more damning circumstances!

Poor Mrs Harris, a tense, and, for heaven's sake, completely undangerous woman, is now leading a wretched life in a high security prison at the expense of the New York taxpayers, all because of a heel, her own scruples, the ridiculous availability of handguns in America, and the adversary system at law.

*Part six*
# MULTIPLE MURDERS
# FOR MONEY

# 1

# Kate Bender

'Pike's Peak or bust!' was the cry of the would-be settlers making their way across America to the cheap land offered by government to homesteaders on the frontier. Quite a number of them did bust. And a hazard that busted twenty or more was Bender's Hotel in Kansas.

Hotel? It was a shack. A plain wood-frame building of crude planking, about 24 ft long by 16 ft wide. There were no interior walls, but a heavy canvas curtain divided it into two sections. The main room was a rough 16 ft square containing shelves with groceries, a counter and a stove. Behind the curtain was the narrow sleeping and eating compartment. It held a long narrow table and four ticking mattresses (stored on top of each other during the day). There were no chairs. Only a bench jammed between the table and the canvas curtain.

John or Johann Bender put the establishment together in 1871. A primitive makeshift place for picking up some stores, filling up with some coarse food, and catching a night's sleep in dirty overcrowded surroundings. A good example of the crude reality underlying the glamorous myths of the old frontier and the Wild West.

It was well situated, close to the trail running west to the Arkansas River, about a day's journey out of Independence. Most travellers would stop and overnight in that reasonably developed town. Then another day rolling westward would land them in godforsaken open prairie, with only the cabins of homesteaders at distances of a mile or more to be seen. Bender's Grocery and Overnight Stop might be unsalubrious, but it was a roof and it offered a cooked meal.

Inside the establishment, three-quarters of the proprietorial family were as unprepossessing as their surroundings. John Bender was a dark, spare crouching man of uncertain age. He had no whiskers according to the Governor's Proclamation ultimately issued for his arrest; but neighbouring homesteaders recalled him as a man whose grizzled black beard covered his face almost up to the eyes. He spoke hardly any English and passed most of his time in front of the hotel studying a German Bible. To most of his neighbours, his occasional utterances in German were just so much guttural grunting. Like any frontiersman, he was decisively aged by his sixty years.

His wife was a fat frau with a trace of dark moustache. She spoke a little broken English, but not often. Most of the time she was busy about the daily tasks of the frontierswoman: cleaning the stove; cooking the heavy greasy food that would have sickened dieticians and gourmets alike; selling the odd grocery staples without seeming to care whether purchases were made or not; letting in travellers or would-be diners with a surliness that could not be called a welcome.

This unlovely couple's son, John Jr, inherited the dark hair and grey eyes that marked both his parents. He had his father's spare frame and height of 5 ft 8 ins or so. At twenty-seven he was blessed with a thin moustache. And he could speak English fluently, though with a pronounced German accent. His conversational flow was interrupted by a constant and annoying nervous giggle. Once he and his father had erected the shack, and dug a small, but obviously very reliable, tornado shelter underneath it, he was hardly ever seen doing any work again.

The saving grace of the Benders lay in the daughter. While her lumpish parents had christened her Johanna, thus severely limiting the variety of Christian names in a family that already contained two Johanns, she had renamed herself Kate. In 1872 she elaborated this to 'Professor Miss Katie Bender', and posted up notices all over Labette County, Kansas, declaring that she could, 'heal all sorts of diseases; can cure blindness, Fits, Deafness and all such diseases, also Deaf and Dumbness.' Any patients coming for treatment would find that she was also a spiritualist medium,

claiming to receive messages and guidance from a departed
redskin chief who had fallen in love with her.

The dead Indian had many living rivals in the surrounding
territory. For out of this uncouth and inarticulate family, Kate
shone like a finely cut diamond. Her English was fluent and only
lightly accented, and ranged from the charmingly playful to a salty
Billingsgate that other settler girls never dared. Her hair was a
deep, deep auburn; black from a distance; glinting with copper and
chestnut lights from close-up. Her complexion was clean and
smooth; a creamy white beautifully merging into rosy cheeks. Her
figure was lithe and supple; its carriage urgent and vital, marked
by what beholders again and again agreed was a 'tigerish grace'.
Kate was beautiful. She was intensely attractive to men and she
knew it. She was quite willing to make love to the local yokels who
swarmed about her, provided they carried out useful tasks on her
behalf.

For Kate – Professor Miss Katie, forsooth! – was as ambitious
as that self-bestowed title suggests. Though only twenty-three
when she came to Kansas (and looking several years younger)
she dominated her family, and no one who knew them doubted
that it was she who called the shots, and established the way in
which the ramshackle hotel was made to earn some thousands of
dollars (unlikely as that seems) in the three short years it was
open.

Kate made no secret of her ambitions. She wanted a lot of
money. And she wanted to be a famous lecturer. The unfocused
immaturity of these wishes was not apparent to the besotted youth
of Labette County. Kate's spritualist claims and attempted faith
healing passed as evidence of intellectual distinction in her social
circles. Her beauty, vitality and downright sexiness made young
men happy to envisage her becoming rich as well.

But how was she going about acquiring the riches? We have one
witness, and one only, who seems to point reliably to the Bender
Hotel's *modus operandi* and Kate's controlling role therein. A Mrs
Fitts lent the family a side-saddle on one occasion. Like several
other settlers in this region, she had German connections, and this
may have made her unusually sympathetic to the antisocial
grocer-innkeepers. When she went to the hotel to fetch her saddle
back, Kate asked her in for a cup of tea. Mrs Fitts accepted, and sat
obligingly on the bench with her back to the canvas curtain. Kate
and old Frau Bender talked amiably with her while they drank

their tea, until, for no reason at all, Kate suddenly interjected, 'Now!'

Nothing happened, and the conversation continued. A few minutes later, Kate said again, urgently, 'Now! Now!' And from the front room, on the other side of the canvas curtain, came old Bender's voice, muttering back in German, 'No – no – by God! I can't do it.'

Mrs Fitts felt the situation had become uncomfortable, but she had no idea why. Nor could she fathom what Mr Bender found himself unable to do, despite his daughter's urging. She was embarrassed at apparently intruding on some private peculiarity, and soon made an excuse to leave. A year later she would know she had been lucky to do so.

In 1872 the territory was becoming disturbed by rumours of a number of disappearances. People back east were complaining that relatives who set off on the long journey to the frontier passed Independence, and suddenly vanished. People from the west were complaining that the Osage Mission seemed to be a boundary from which no eastbound travellers returned. The country was not especially dangerous. There was Indian territory nearby, but the Indians were not in revolt. The prairies were bare and lightly cultivated, but they were not a desert. There seemed no reason for people to go missing in this peaceful district of scattered homesteaders and hayseed stockhands.

The little hamlets of Parsons and Cherry Vale began to win an unhealthy reputation when two bodies were found floating in the Verdigris river, their throats cut and the backs of their heads stove in. A third was found in similar condition out on the prairie near Oswego. Neighbours suspected neighbours of practising highway robbery and murder. But no more bodies were found in the open, though the disappearance of travellers was still reported. Coincidentally, a new law had just been passed prohibiting stockholders from dumping dead cattle out on the prairie. It didn't occur to anyone at this point that this would make a flock of vultures an interesting and relatively unusual spectacle, instead of a familiar and disgusting sight pointing only to abandoned ox-carrion and bones.

Then in 1873 a well-known and important man with a powerful family disappeared. Dr York of Independence journeyed west to visit his brother, Colonel York, at Fort Scott. When he hadn't returned home three weeks later, Mrs York wrote to her brother-in-law, and the Colonel instantly formed a posse. He was a Civil War veteran, and like many frontier soldiers, a skilled scout who knew other expert trackers. Among his fifty or sixty cowhands and roustabouts were former commissioned officers who knew as much as any men living about following a trail, and this deadly little army set out to scour the sixty miles between Fort Scott and Independence.

The Colonel was a prominent local citizen, and in the running for election as State Senator. No one refused to answer his questions, and he easily traced the doctor's movements from Osage Mission to Cherry Vale and on to the Bender Hotel. The Benders, too, remembered their visitor. He had stayed overnight and departed in the morning. Miss Kate offered to try and find him through her redskin spirit guide. Young John suggested that the doctor might have been attacked by bandits, and told an unlikely story of having been shot at himself by a sniper hiding behind a sapling at Drum Creek. The Colonel put them down as well-meaning but over-anxious to seem helpful, probably in the anticipation of some reward. Only Jimmy Buster, one of the men riding with him, thought the Benders seemed suspicious. The Colonel pooh-poohed this idea, and the posse continued to search a trail which suddenly went cold.

Three days later, two men called Toles and Roach who shared an interest in sexy Miss Kate, passed by the hotel and noticed that a cow was starving in its pen. Closer investigation showed that the Benders' pigs had not been fed and were eating each other's tails. A closer search still, and it was apparent that the Benders had disappeared, leaving their cabin empty.

Colonel York and the posse came back to investigate this new and really shocking disappearance of an entire family in the mystery district. One look into the underground tornado shelter, reached by a trapdoor under the dining-table, proved that the Benders were villains, not victims. It stank to high heaven. The stone slab and coarse gravel at its base were heavy with congealed and putrefied blood. The narrow underground escape passage out to the Benders' land showed signs of bodies having been dragged along it. And the Benders' land contained shallow depressions suggesting recent graves.

Eleven bodies were recovered. Almost all had been killed by a heavy blow which smashed in the backs of their heads, followed by throat-cutting. A sledge-hammer and a maul found in the

Benders' front room were obviously the weapons. Kate's urgent,
'Now!' was the signal for her father to strike through the canvas
when the victim's head was touching it and his attention was
distracted. Mrs Fitts had been saved, either because wicked old
Johann could not bring himself to murder an elderly lady, or more
probably because he was less greedy than Kate, and realized that
the disappearance of a neighbour who had come to collect her
property from the Benders would throw instant suspicion on the
family.

Most of the eleven bodies on the property belonged to solitary
men who had stopped at the hotel. They included Dr York. But
there was one married couple, and it seemed that the Benders had
first killed the husband in their normal way, and then the two
Johanns had raped the wife before cutting her throat. And there
was a man called Longcor who had been struck with the hammer,
thrown in the cellar and had his throat cut, like everyone else, and
then, after he had been pitched into his waiting grave, his little
nine-year-old daughter had been thrown in after him and buried
alive. A Cherry Vale housewife cut off the dead child's long blonde
hair and made a wreath of it. It can still be seen at the bizarre
Bender Museum in Kansas, beside the hammer that struck her
father down.

The Benders had disappeared, and from that day to this they
have never been reliably seen again. They had realized over
$4,000, plus a couple of wagons and horses and a good deal of
personal jewellery from the eleven buried on their land alone. How
much more they had previously made from unknown victims
thrown into the river and onto the prairie will never be known.
They were cunning enough to keep their ill-gotten wealth hidden.
Were they also cunning enough to escape?

There were frequent reports that old John had been seen in
Michigan, where he was said to have committed suicide. Two
women were arrested up there thirteen years later, and charged
with being Frau Bender and Kate. They weren't. Kate was
subsequently said to have been seen working in a New Orleans
brothel. That story is so unlikely that you might as well suggest
that she lived to the ripe old age of 123 and at last let Lord Lucan
into her successful hiding place!

No. Local deathbed confessions in Kansas made by members of
Colonel York's posse suggest a likelier end. Detectives trailed the
Benders to the railway, where they bought tickets for Humboldt,

but left the train at Chanute and struck out for Indian territory. Cunning. But not the wisest move with old trackers like Colonel York and his men on their trail.

I suspect that the deathbed confessions were true. That the Benders were overtaken by the posse of vigilantes who slaughtered them with as little mercy as they had shown their victims, weighted the bodies, and threw them into a river with their bellies ripped open so that the interior gases would escape and they would never float up and impede Colonel York's political career. And, much as I dislike lynch law, I can't say that I feel as disapproving as I ought, when I remember the raped wife and the little Longcor girl. Anyway, the Bender family were the last people to vanish so mysteriously from the sinister section of trail between Independence and Osage Mission.

# 2

# Herman Webster Mudgett

Herman Webster Mudgett. Could one invent a more prosaic name? Yet it is the name of one of the most colourful criminals of all time. A man who traded in corpses in America sixty years after the bodysnatching business had been firmly terminated in England. A fraudster wanted for horse-stealing in Texas. A lover who disposed effectively and finally of discarded mistresses, yet spared the women who married him, legitimately or bigamously. The creator of an amazing Bluebeard's Castle in Chicago, where he trapped and murdered an unknown number of hotel guests during the World's Fair of 1893. An evil genius whose final confession stated, 'I was born with the devil in me. I could not help the fact that I was a murderer, no more than a poet can help the inspiration to song. I was born with the evil one standing as my sponsor beside the bed where I was ushered into the world, and he has been with me ever since.'

The evil one kept this appointment at Gilmanton, New Hampshire in 1860. Mudgett was genuinely a man of the highest ability. He qualified as a doctor in 1884, but was only able to practise from 1885 to 1886. For in that year, Dr Mudgett of Mooers Forks, New York, deserted his wife and son; absconded to Chicago; and took up a new life under a new name. As H. H. Holmes, he bigamously married Myrta Belknap. And clearly a Dr Holmes could not open a practice based on the qualifications and certificates given to a Dr Mudgett. He started divorce proceedings to separate himself from his real wife, Clara Lovering Mudgett, but never followed them through.

Holmes (as we must call him from now on) started to live by his wits. He borrowed money to build himself a home in the Chicago suburb of Wilmette, secured against a note signed by Myrta's Uncle Jonathan. Wanting yet more ready cash, he forged another note from Uncle Jonathan, and when he was found out, charmingly invited his wife's uncle to come and inspect the new house from the roof. Uncle Jonathan wisely declined, and became one of the minority who survived the experience of being cheated by Holmes. Nor did he press charges against his niece's husband for forgery and fraud.

In 1888 Holmes took a job as a pharmacist in Englewood, a suburb on the opposite side of Chicago from Wilmette. His employer was a Mrs Holden. In 1890, as if by magic, her drugstore suddenly turned out to be the property of H. H. Holmes. Mrs Holden accused Holmes of embezzlement and fraudulent accounting to bring the business into his personal possession. She clearly intended to fight the case, but before she could start proceedings, she disappeared. Holmes said she had decided to travel through California. She was never heard of again. Convenient for Holmes.

Equally convenient was the possession of business premises at a considerable distance from his wife and home. Holmes took a flat above the shop and used it for the womanizing which was to prove a marked feature of his life.

Around this time, a jeweller called Icilius Corner came to Chicago with his wife and family, and reached an agreement with Holmes whereby he took in watch repairs at the drugstore. Icilius's eighteen-year-old sister-in-law, Gertie, took a secretarial post, helping Holmes with his new mail-order business. This consisted of marketing two classic American 'snake-oil' type quack remedies: capsules of bismuth and sugar guaranteed as a certain and complete cure for alcoholism, and a preparation of sweet spirits of nitre in tea as a cure for baldness.

And in the flat above the shop, Gertie sported with Holmes as the occasion arose. So did her sister, Icilius's wife Julia.

In 1892 Icilius discovered what was going on. He promptly divorced Julia and went back to Iowa. Holmes was suddenly left with Gertie, Julia and Julia's little daughter Pearl all dependent on him.

Julia was the most difficult of the three. Unlike Myrta on the other side of town, she objected to her man's constant womanizing. Holmes devised his first domestic architectural innovation, concealing the button for an electric buzzer under the carpet outside Julia's room, so that he was warned whenever she left the confines of her sanctum. Then either Gertie or sixteen-year-old Emily van Tassell from the fruitshop down the road could be hastily extricated from his embrace, and sent on her way.

It soon became apparent that Gertie was pregnant. When she disappeared, Holmes told everyone she had gone home to Iowa. When nothing more was heard from her, Holmes told everyone he had received a letter saying that she had died.

'Holmes!' cried a friend of his, for all the world like Dr Watson, 'You have killed her!' But H. H. Holmes laughed the accusation off and went on his way.

In June Emily van Tassell disappeared. Holmes offered no explanation for once.

In the autumn he took on a new secretary. Beautiful blonde Emmeline Cigrand helped, among other things, with a patent invention Holmes was using to raise cash. This was a wonderful machine that turned plain tapwater into household gas. The machine looked like an immense washing-machine on stilts, bristling with impressive pipes and pressure gauges. When Holmes filled it with water and added a secret chemical component, gas was emitted from a tap and could be ignited for demonstration purposes. Many people invested in this remarkable invention, only to be disappointed when they learned that it worked only because one of the many pipes ran directly from the gas main to the gas tap.

Julia objected to Emmeline. Julia and her daughter disappeared.

A couple of months later Emmeline disappeared, too. Gone into a convent, Holmes explained.

His new secretary, Texan Methodist Minnie Williams, dominated Holmes's private life at the time of his greatest creation. Foreseeing the influx of visitors to the Chicago World's Fair of 1893, Holmes bought a large building lot opposite the drugstore, and built a vast three-storey hotel with shops at ground level. He didn't, of course, do anything so mundane as paying for the building. He simply ordered the workmen off the lot and hired new builders every time a contractor was insensitive enough to ask for money. This had the added advantage that nobody except Holmes ever saw the plans for the entire building. Only he knew the secrets hidden within the most amazing Bluebeard's Castle ever created.

The first to be put into use was a windowless room in the heart of the building. Holmes ordered furnishings on credit, and then told the company they had never arrived. The company disbelieved him, and sent in bailiffs to recover their property. But the bailiffs were quite unable to find it. Holmes had it packed ceiling-high in the windowless room, and then plastered over the door.

A cunning trick. But equally useful were the passages that ended in surprising cul-de-sacs; the secret passages from one room to another; the complete set of electric buzzer buttons outside all rooms which meant that Holmes, sitting like a spider in his control-room, could tell exactly which of his guests were or were not in their rooms. Rooms which were all made airtight and could be filled with gas at the turn of a tap. . . .

There were two levels of basements beneath the shops. Connected with the hotel rooms by two large greased chutes. In the basements were tables on which, should anyone wish to do such a thing, bodies might be cut up. And a large furnace in which, should anyone have such things on hand, dismembered bodies might be consumed. . . .

A lot of people stayed at Mr Holmes's hotel during the Chicago World's Fair. And a number of his guests never emerged again. Mr Holmes made a tidy little profit on the year, breaking his business venture only for one domestic interlude in June, when Minnie Williams's sister Nancy came on a visit. It seemed that Nancy stood between Minnie and the sole ownership of some valuable property in Texas. Nancy disappeared.

At the end of the World's Fair Mr Holmes's hotel caught fire. It was not destroyed, but Mr Holmes put in a sizeable claim for insurance. The adjusters accused him of arson. The many creditors and gulls who wanted an urgent word with Mr H. H. Holmes (or Harry Gordon, or H. S. Campbell – all names he had used in his various frauds) gathered for the kill. Holmes fled. Minnie disappeared. Holmes was to tell anyone who cared about this that she had run away to escape the charge of murdering her sister Nancy in the summer!

From Chicago, Holmes went to Fort Worth, where he intended to appropriate that property Minnie had inherited.

Now, for a couple of years Holmes had been employing a broken-down alcoholic carpenter named Benjamin Fuller Pitezel as an accomplice. Pitezel was a competent workman when sober, but he had a large family, and was prepared to live by his wits. He

had passed forged cheques and acted as a go-between in having the
hotel erected, and on the one occasion when he had been caught
and gaoled to await trial for forgery, Holmes intervened in the
guise of a passing Indiana congressman, and secured Pitezel's
release on bail with another forged cheque!

Pitezel now became an active assistant in the recovery of
Minnie's Fort Worth property. The pair promptly used it,
fraudulently, as security for large loans. One of these was used for
the further fraudulent purchase of horses. So Holmes was now a
horse thief. Still a hanging matter in Texas, only twenty years
away from the heyday of the Wild West. He fled back north.

With him went his third 'wife', innocent and honest Georgiana
Yoak, who would only consent to sleep with a husband. From now
on his past and furture crimes had to be concealed from her.

His next venture was an elaborate insurance racket. Mr Pitezel
insured his life for a large sum, and then went to Philadelphia and
established himself as a patent agent under the name of B. F.
Perry.

Holmes, for the first and only time in his life, was caught out by
the law in a minor fraud, and gaoled for two weeks in St Louis,
where Georgiana bailed him out. In prison, Holmes asked burglar
Marion Hedgepeth for the name of a good crooked lawyer.
Hedgepeth recommended one Jephthah D. Howe, and Holmes
promised him a share of the ultimate proceeds of the fraud in
return.

The scheme was complicated. Pitezel was to get hold of a fresh
corpse. (Holmes ran a lucrative side-line in procuring corpses for
surgical and anatomical laboratories.) Holmes would then doctor
it in a way known to him, to make it appear the almost
unrecognizable victim of an explosion. Pitezel as 'B. F. Perry'
would establish a small local reputation for home chemistry, and
would then disappear. The doctored corpse would be found in his
laboratory, apparently the victim of an accident. Howe would then
come forward to suggest that the body might be his missing client
B. F. Pitezel. Holmes, as a family friend would identify it, and one
of Pitezel's children would confirm the identification. The
insurance company would pay out to Mrs Pitezel, who had thus
been completely distanced from both the death and the identification. And Holmes, Pitezel, Hedgepeth and Howe would split the
proceeds.

It worked like a charm. Pitezel's twelve-year-old daughter was particularly convincing in her tearful recognition of the corpse as her father. Holmes made only one mistake. He reneged on his promise to pay Hedgepeth, and the burglar blew the whistle on the scheme.

By the time the police had worked out that the body in Philadelphia really *was* Pitezel, and Holmes had lethally cheated his principal accomplice, Holmes and the Pitezel family had disappeared. In fact, Holmes spent the next few months in a sequence of brilliant manoeuvres to transport Mrs Pitezel, the Pitezel children and Georgiana Yoak into obscurity, travelling as three separate and parallel parties, without any of them suspecting that the other two existed. Mrs Pitezel could not be allowed to meet her daughter and learn that it really *was* Daddy who lay dead in Philadelphia. Georgiana Yoak was not to know of any nefarious activities at all.

So Holmes managed to shepherd his three flocks from St Louis to Cincinnati; to Indianapolis; to Detroit and to Toronto. There the three parties were reduced to two. He had already suffocated young Howard Pitezel in Indiana. Now he murdered his sisters in Canada.

The survivors went on to Ogdensburg, New York; to Burlington, Vermont (where Holmes complicated his life yet further by making an emotional reconciliation with his first and genuine wife); and on to Boston. There at last, Pinkerton's man Richard Geyer who had been tailing him and uncovering children's bodies *en route*, caught up with the villain.

Holmes was taken back to Philadelphia and convicted of poisoning Pitezel with chloroform before doctoring the body to make it look like the victim of an accident. Holmes performed brilliantly at his trial, but the evidence was too strong against him.

Before his execution he confessed to the repeated assassinations of his surplus women, and said he had killed thirteen visitors to his Chicago hotel. The most extreme estimate of more cynical investigators places his score of victims at well over a hundred.

The outraged citizenry burned that wonderful building down, alas. Since its plans were always in Holmes's head, we cannot today create a replica of the most remarkable house in the history of crime.

# 3

## Susanna Olah

Peasant communities are hard and thrifty. Poor peasant communities, living close to subsistence level, know that extra mouths to feed may mean hunger and sickness for everyone. Catholic peasant communities will not practise birth control. And in avoiding the lesser sin may fall into a greater.

Susanna Olah's remarkable achievement was to lead her village communities past abortion and into mass murder. While other villains may have killed more victims more cruelly, Susanna can surely claim one record. No one has ever led so many law-abiding neighbours into the calm and habitual practice of murder. After Susanna's death, thirty-one women from the twin villages of Tiszakurt and Nagyrev faced murder charges. Only great evil philosophies like Fascism have exceeded Susanna in precipitating mass moral decline.

In 1905 Susanna began to practise midwifery in the little villages of the Hungarian wine-growing lands. They were only sixty miles from Budapest, but snows in winter and floods in spring often isolated them. The sturdy villagers were well placed to become a law unto themselves.

Susanna was not the only midwife in Tiszakurt and Nagyrev. But she was a good one. And she offered one service which the others refused. She would procure abortions for favoured patients. The farmers' wives welcomed this handy and economic service. Susanna's practice grew and her influence increased proportionately.

Shortly before the Great War, Susanna saw the possibility of
offering another service. Wives who had imprudently failed to take
advantage of her secret abortions and found themselves landed
with unwanted additions to the family could yet be helped. Aunt
Susanna (as she was now known) had one useful functionary under
her influence. The village bellringer was also the registrar of births,
marriages and deaths. He had married Susanna's daughter, and
was close enough to the Olah family to be prevented from asking
awkward questions if the infant mortality rate took a small leap.
Susanna began storing arsenic, acquired by soaking those
arsenical flypapers so popular with murderers around the turn of
the century. A little dose to the poor little mite (who could
conceivably have starved to death, anyway) and the overburdened
parents could rest assured that the family food budget remained
within manageable control. And Suzanna's patients were now
involved in something more serious than abortion. Her control
over the villages' womenfolk tightened accordingly.

One group was impervious to her skills and offers. The
respectable midwives disliked having an abortionist working
among them. Susanna found herself reported to the authorities
and charged on a couple of occasions. Both times she beat the rap,
and the experience only served to convince her that she was
impervious to legal sanctions. She felt, too, that hostile competition was something a good midwife-abortionist-baby-murderer
could do without. Little packets of arsenic would work on people
who were more than a few months old. A mysterious tummy-bug
started to strike down the midwives of Tiszakurt and Nagyrev.
Only Susanna Olah proved immune to it. By the time the Great
War opened she was unthreatened by professional competition.

But the strange deaths of midwives accompanied by the no less
strange survival of Mrs Olah prompted sinister speculation and
suspicion among the men of the villages. They were not privy to
their wives' secrets of population control, and had no real idea why
the midwife living among them was coming to exert so much
influence over their womenfolk. But witchcraft might obviously be
suspected. Anyway, it would be a good thing if all farmers' wives
had a great deal less to do with Aunt Susanna. Several patriarchal
husbands absolutely banned any association with her. This was a
mistake.

Having eliminated the competition, Susanna was now the
principal medical authority in the villages at such times as weather

cut them off from the outside world. There simply had to be communication with her if there was sickness in the family. Susanna learned of the interdict, and her response was a move of the utmost political brilliance.

Put very simply, she invented radical sexual feminism out of her own head and invited her supporters among the village women to join with her in solemn league and covenant. They demanded full sexual equality with their husbands. Freedom to refuse their advances at will. Freedom to take outside lovers of their own. It was a heady offer of liberation, and it worked instantly. Cowed wives realized that Aunt Susanna's proposals, put into practice by the united womenfolk of the two villages, offered them new freedom, independence and dignity. Quite enough women were prepared to support the programme to ensure that Mrs Olah had her full share of cronies – disciples, even.

Now I'd better put my cards on the table quite frankly. I approve entirely of the family reforms Susanna Olah devised and put into practice. I am happy to have come of age in the 'permissive' 1960s, and would willingly extend the unfettered freedom of that happy and optimistic decade to everyone else on earth. I am delighted to think that for ten years, two villages full of peasant women were free to refuse their husbands' coarse coupling if they chose, and equally free to enjoy such pleasures as they could find with lusty youths, even as their husbands might frolic with nubile wenches. It's not the fact that Susanna started a women's movement that worries me, nor the fact that the Church fathers feared that godly family life seemed to be lapsing into anarchy in two tiny communities of otherwise conservative peasants. What worries me more than a little is the kind of sanction Susanna applied to ensure that recalcitrant husbands did not inhibit their wives' growth to adult independence and responsibility.

For there was, of course, resistance. Who can doubt that wives were beaten; wives were locked out; wives were punished and humiliated for opposing the demands of their lords and masters. But Susanna had the answer to that. And the camouflage for its social consequences. A little packet of arsenic, sprinkled generously over food or in drink proved sovereign in terminating chronic cases of wife-beating. Arsenic was better than bromide for ensuring that marital rape never took place in the best bedroom. The leaders of male chauvinist resistance proved strangely sickly. One by one the leading anti-feminists of Nagyrev and Tiszakurt died off. The compliant bellringer entered the deaths without a murmer in his register. And, as Susanna shrewdly calculated, no skilful statistician paid any attention to a sudden leap in the adult male death rate in the middle of the bloodiest war in human history. Her villages' population graph simply wandered a little more steeply along the line of bloodshed staining the whole of Europe.

By the end of the war Susanna had perfectly emasculated the two villages. The women ruled, and it was okay by them. The hen-pecked survived and, perhaps, those few who genuinely accepted that their wives were entitled to full private equality with themselves.

But now a new concern came to dominate the poisoning. Property. Susanna's reforms had not touched the unequal distribution of wealth between landowning men and their dependent wives. But widows could own farms. . . . And peasant women who had cast longing eyes on pieces of land that weren't up for sale . . . widows who didn't like seeing their husbands' entailed land pass away to nephews . . . ladies who had waited longer than seemed decent for an inheritance to come their way . . . all these could find answers to their problems in the little packages of arsenic. Huge quantities of wealth as measured by land-hungry smallholders began changing hands in consequence of a new rash of sudden deaths in the little villages.

In 1929 one of the league of free women made a mistake. She had a pair of troublesome old relatives – many of us do. They died very conveniently. And the rumour that she had poisoned them came to the ear of the parish priest.

Now the Church's inflexible sexual moral code, rigidly enforced by uncomprehending celibates, had ensured that no word of poisoning for liberated pleasures ever came to its austere ears. But property is another matter. In quarrelling over land, money and inheritances, the Church has always proved itself a whopping great sinner, along with the best of us. So it could easily be whispered in the good Father's ear that there was something a little convenient about that particular death, wasn't there . . .? The good Father taxed the suspected poisoner with the allegations.

Bursting with virtuous indignation, the good lady invited the priest to come to her home and discuss the whole matter over a dish of tea. He did so. The explanation was not very good. The tea was even worse. It made him violently sick.

Alas, Susanna's pupil had miscalculated her dose and her man. The priest did not die, and he had no doubt what had caused his temporary disorder. The good lady was arrested and charged with attempted poisoning. Once she was behind bars, the question of her relatives could be taken up as well. And, isolated from the protective ranks of the sisterhood, she broke and admitted that the useful little packets of powder came from Aunt Susanna Olah, who was well known to supply them when they were needed.

The authorities proceeded to question Susanna forthwith. She was sharply intelligent. She knew when there was too large a volume of crime known to too many accomplices for escape to prove possible. I'd like to think that if only her sexual libertarianism had been at stake, she might have stood up proudly to be counted a martyr to male chauvinism. But baby poisoning is far less sympathetic. And by the time of her arrest . . . well . . . avarice seemed to be the main motive behind all the poisonings. Susanna killed herself.

The enquiry uncovered a really amazing quantity of murder in the villages. At least a hundred unnatural deaths had occurred (an average of ten a year through Queen Susanna's unofficial reign.) Thirty-one women were arrested, of whom five effectively confessed their guilt (or their discipleship) by killing themselves. All were convicted. Several were hanged. And they serve to remind the most active political idealists that noble ends can never justify murderous and uncontrollable means.

# Epilogue

Well, there you have them. Thirty-three of the 'Murders After Midnight' that I've enjoyed most. And a few words you've never heard before, even if you've listened regularly. The sort of words that bring protests from lonely listeners, who don't like to turn on the radio at 1.15 in the morning and hear gory details of unbridled lust and savagery.

I've tried to be careful in what I say late at night, after the screams of protest over Michael De Freitas. (Though if protesters care to check the script here, they'll see that I was not exaggerating when I said that the part they dislike is about one twelfth of a script which focuses intensely on political and social morality.)

Yet even while editing this set of scripts for publication, I've upset listeners again with too precise a description of Ed Kemper's nasty habits. I expected that script to raise a few eyebrows for the remark, (apropos Kemper's blushing modesty toward a girl he was about to butcher and ravish), that 'the conservative Judaeo-Christian sexual ethic is mad, bad and dangerous to attempt'. But Clive Bull, my gentle presenter says no, we are all very generous about free-thinking opinions, but being part of Eliot's humankind, cannot bear very much reality. Some listeners didn't like knowing about the butchery.

This book describes reality I hope you cannot bear. For murder can truly be most foul. Yet it continues to happen. And to fascinate. And if you enjoy reading about it and improving your moral sensitivity by adjudging it, then you have more to look forward to. For I continue to report on murders, old and new, at home and abroad: Ed Kemper ... Lord Erroll ... Psycho Eddy ... Jay Smith ... Bible John ... Captain Margary ... Mark Essex ... Walton the Witch ... Sellers the Schoolboy Satanist ... Little Willie Starchfield ... Bonnie and Clyde ... the Rainbow Warrior ... Lucrezia Borgia ....